PATRIARCHS, MATRIARCHS, AND ANARCHS

Genesis 12–50

A 13-WEEK STUDY WITH

Dr. Tony W. Cartledge

THE *Nurturing*
FAITH™
BIBLE STUDY SERIES

© 2018
Published in the United States by Nurturing Faith Inc., Macon GA,
www.nurturingfaith.net.

Library of Congress Cataloging-in-Publication Data is available.

ISBN 978-1-63528-040-1

Abbreviations

KJV	King James Version
HCSB	Holman Christian Standard Bible
NET	New English Translation (also known as the NETBible)
LXX	Septuagint, an early Greek translation of the Old Testament
MT	Masoretic Text, the "standard" Hebrew text of the Old Testament
NASB	New American Standard Bible, 1977 edition
NAS95	New American Standard Bible, 1995 edition
NET	The NETBible, New English Translation, 1996-2017
NIV	New International Version, 1984 edition
NIV11	New International Version, 2011 edition
NRSV	New Revised Standard Version

Cover photo by Tony Cartledge
The Hill of Moreh rises above the Jezreel Valley, where Abraham reportedly made his
first camp upon entering the land of Canaan.

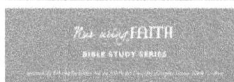

Other resources from

Nurturing Faith
BOOKS

CONTENTS

PREFACE

B ible study is a discipline that calls for the engagement of both hearts and minds. The Nurturing Faith Bible Series is designed to focus attention on biblical texts that expand the mind and enrich the heart.

Dr. Tony Cartledge brings the insights of a scholar, the heart of a pastor, and the communication skills of a seasoned writer and editor to this important task. With careful scholarship he guides learners to a clearer understanding of the context—language, culture, and setting—in which the biblical accounts occurred.

Then the important question is considered, "How do these ancient words speak to us as people of faith today?" Truth—not bound by time and culture—awaits those who are willing to dig, contemplate, and apply these biblical treasures.

Respecting the need to engage scripture with both heart and mind, there is no attempt to "dumb down" the lessons or to ignore the challenges of serious inquiry. This is a distinguishing mark of the Nurturing Faith Bible Study Series

Therefore, each lesson concludes with "The Hardest Question" in which Dr. Cartledge both raises and responds to such challenges in understanding and applying the biblical revelation to today's living.

An honest wrangling with the biblical revelation—while guided by God's Spirit—can produce clearer understanding and stronger commitments. Such Bible study will indeed nurture one's faith.

These lessons explore the spiritual ancestors revealed in the book of Genesis—providing insights into their evolving faith. Digging into these studies will help answer the two-fold question: Who were these people, and what do their lives have to do with mine?

May these 13 sessions of exploring inspired biblical texts bring new insights and a refreshed commitment to living faithfully today as followers of God who is revealed most fully in Jesus Christ.

John D. Pierce, Publisher
Nurturing Faith, Inc.

This volume in the Nurturing Faith Bible Study Series
is made possible through a generous gift
from Lynda and Dan Bryson, given in memory of
Charles Pittard and in honor of Joy Pittard.

***

Nurturing Faith seeks sponsors for future volumes in this Bible study series.
To inquire, please contact office@nurturingfaith.net.

INTRODUCTION

Few parts of the Bible have occasioned as much interest and commentary as Genesis 12–50. Traditionally, it has been called the "Patriarchal History," in contrast to the "Primeval History" of Genesis 1–11. In recent years, many scholars have chosen to avoid the male-dominant implications of "Patriarchal History" and refer to Genesis 12–50 as "Stories of the Ancestors." In the studies that comprise this book, we will consider the roles of both patriarchs and matriarchs as players in the story of the promise—and how both could also act as anarchs whose actions seemed to threaten the promise, but were ultimately woven into the complex tapestry of Israel's many-layered story of origins.

As we read, we must keep in mind that Genesis 12–50 was written by Israel and for Israel. More specifically, its final form was shaped by someone from the southern kingdom of Judah who sought to magnify the tribe of Judah—and younger sons—from the beginning. The people of Judah were conquered by the Babylonians in 587 BCE, and many of them carried into a faith-shaking period of exile. After Cyrus the Persian conquered Babylon in 539 BCE, he allowed the Israelites to return to Jerusalem and the surrounding area shortly thereafter, but still as subjects of the Persian Empire.

Religious and political leaders realized that the Hebrews were no longer in a position to be an independent kingdom or nation, but they could still be preserved as a people. Seizing on that idea, they put increasing stress on a belief that the Hebrews, from the time of Abraham, had been the chosen people of God, called to be set apart for Yahweh (God's personal name as revealed in the Old Testament), even if they lived as a minority people in a small sub-province called Yehud (an Aramaic spelling of Judah). The people of Yehud were Yehudim, a name that morphed into what Western languages came to pronounce as "Jews."

In this process, then, the Hebrews became Jews, inheritors of a promise given first to Abraham, and later to Isaac and Jacob, both of whom are chosen over their older brothers. The family line carried on through the male descendants of Abraham forms the skeleton of traditions on which Genesis 12–50 was framed, and the foundation upon which the traditions of Israel's history were built.

Two appendices offer a guide to finding our way through the family maze of Abraham and his many relations, many of whom are said to have become the ancestors of Israel's later enemies. By examining these convoluted relationships, we can see just how big and interconnected the biblical writers considered Israel's family to be.

In these studies we will also see how jumbled and confusing a story can be when it is composed from multiple sources that rely on oral traditions passed down over a very long period of time. All but the most diehard conservative scholars concluded long ago that Moses could not have written the Pentateuch, though the first five books of the Hebrew Bible were often called the "books of Moses." Moses was the main character in four of the five books, but could hardly have written them. Not only do the books record Moses' death and what came after (Deut. 34:5ff), but there are also clear signs of writing styles, vocabulary, and distinctive views of God that point to several different sources.

While various scholars may take slightly different approaches, it is common to speak of most patriarchal narratives as deriving from a source called the "Yahwist" (or "J"), because it has a clearly Judean perspective and commonly calls God by the name "Yahweh" (nearly always translated as "LORD," in all caps). Other sources also contribute, including the Elohist (E) source, which prefers to call God "Elohim" and seems to have been written by someone (probably a priest) from the northern kingdom. A source that emphasizes genealogies and cultic matters is generally called the Priestly source (P). It reflects the perspective of Israel's later religious establishment. Priestly writers likely brought the earlier sources together into an edited—but not always unified—whole. A fourth major source, the Deuteronomist (D), is responsible for the Book of Deuteronomy and possibly a few minor edits in the other books.

The J source is normally considered to be the earliest, perhaps as early as the ninth century BCE, with E adding its own stories and editing the work of J about a century later. The Book of Deuteronomy was probably completed just prior to the exile. The P source is commonly credited with adding a great deal of priestly-related traditions and combining the various sources into a carefully edited—if not unified—whole. The long editing process and an aversion to deleting anything from the story led to a number of duplications or different ways of telling the same story.

Structurally, it is obvious that chapters 12–36—composed of short stories that are loosely connected and almost interchangeable—are quite different in character than chapters 37–50, a much lengthier composition with a complex plot that is often labeled "the Joseph novella."

Hermann Gunkel, the pioneer of a field of study we call "form criticism," assigned most of the stories in Genesis 12–50 to the genre called "legend." This term refers to family stories (usually) that may be based on a historical kernel, but have been expanded in the telling and used to pass on unifying beliefs. But, as

Brevard Childs reminds us, the stories have been edited and brought together in a canonical form that has its own theological and didactic purpose.

The stories of the ancestors begin with Abraham (first called Abram) and his wife Sarah (first known as Sarai). Their stories begin with the genealogy of Genesis 11:10-32, which traces Abraham's ancestry to Shem, one of Noah's three sons. The modern term "Semite" derives from "Shem." The stories of Abraham and Sarah extend through the birth of Isaac and beyond, reaching from Genesis 12 to Abraham's death in Genesis 25:11.

Isaac proves to be an unfortunate character, for though he appears often, he is most commonly in the role of Abraham's long-awaited son who didn't get a wife (Rebekah) until his mother died when he was 40, or as Jacob's feeble father who favored Esau but was easily fooled. Isaac is born in Genesis 21 and doesn't die until Genesis 35, but he has center stage only in Genesis 25–27. Even then his adventures mimic those of his father Abraham. When Isaac is old, Jacob comes to the fore by finagling to receive his aged father's blessing by pretending to be his twin brother Esau (Genesis 27). Jacob, along with his four wives, then remains the lead character through Genesis 36. Jacob doesn't die until the end of the book, hovering in the background of the Joseph stories, but Joseph is clearly the focus of Genesis 37–50.

In these studies, which look at sample stories from each of the patriarchal families, it is not our goal to judge whether these interconnected and sometimes contradictory accounts really happened just as the narratives say, but to dig into the purpose of the people who remembered them and the writers who compiled them, hoping to discover what they want us to learn.

Genesis 12:1-9

ON THE ROAD WITH ABRAHAM

I will make of you a great nation,
and I will bless you, and make your name great,
so that you will be a blessing.
—Genesis 12:2

D o you ever give much thought to whether you are in the place God wants you to be? Many people believe that God has laid out a very specific plan for each person's life, and that our job is to be like skilled spiritual detectives who can combine spiritual clues with prayers for guidance to determine just where God wants us to go, what God wants us to do, and who God wants us to marry (if at all).

Other equally devoted believers are less convinced that God has a "perfect plan" for our location and vocation and relationships, but still remain confident that there is one place God wants us to be, and that is in the place of obedience.

If we are obedient, following God may lead to a particular place or job or person, but following God also has to do with the way in which we conduct ourselves, to live as we believe God has called us to live.

There is a story in the Bible that tells us something about what it means to follow God. To find this story, we have to go about as far back as we can go in the biblical story of God's relationship with Israel—all the way back to a home that was not in Israel, but in the southern Mesopotamian land of Sumer.

A RADICAL CALL
(v. 1)

Once upon a time there was a man named Abraham, though he started life with a shorter name, "Abram." Abram grew up in a big exciting city that was already three thousand years old when he was born, and that could have been nearly four thousand years ago. The name of the city was "Ur," and it sat on the banks of the Euphrates River like a queen on her throne. There were no other cities around that could match the city of Ur.

The people of Ur were especially proud of a great temple they called E-temen-ni-guru, a ziggurat built of multiple stories, with each being a little smaller than the one before, so that it resembled a giant, square wedding cake. The temple was dedicated to the moon god, whose Sumerian name was Nanna, and people came from miles around to worship the moon at the great temple of Ur.

> ⚓ **Fertile Crescent:** The term "Fertile Crescent" refers to a crescent-shaped area between the Persian Gulf, where the Tigris and Euphrates rivers entered the sea, up the well-watered region between the two rivers, then west toward the Mediterranean Sea and down through Palestine to Egypt.
>
> The Fertile Crescent skirted the Syrian desert, which was virtually impassable before the domestication of camels, and exceedingly difficult even then, so it was the only reasonable route of travel between Mesopotamia and western countries.

Abram's father Terah acknowledged the moon god as his ancestors did according to Josh. 24:2, and, so far as we know, Abram did, too. He may have seen some impressive ceremonies and sacrifices there, with well-dressed statues of gods being paraded around, but he never heard Nanna speak, unless one of the priests was a ventriloquist.

That's the way it was in Ur, but something told Abram's family that it was time for a change. Terah and Abram and his wife Sarai and his nephew Lot loaded their belongings on a long line of donkeys, and they began to travel northward along one of the well-worn roads that led through the Fertile Crescent. ⚓

The text suggests that they had set out for Canaan (11:31), but instead of continuing west and south, they turned right at the Balikh River, a tributary of the Euphrates, and headed north to the booming Mesopotamian city of Haran, where residents also worshiped the familiar moon god.

Abram's father must have been happy in Haran, because he decided to stay there until he died. Abram and his wife Sarah lived in Haran until Abram was 75 years old, and Sarah was well past retirement age, too.

You might think that people of that age would be ready to retire and settle down, so it's surprising how ready Abram was when the LORD (Yahweh) came to him one day and called his name. We don't know how it is that a man immersed in moon worship for 75 years could suddenly recognize the voice of the real

> ⚜ **A "J" story:** Today's text uses the name Yahweh for God throughout, and portrays Yahweh as speaking directly to Abram without recourse to angels, clouds, or a burning bush. These characteristics, along with the earthy language, identify the text as deriving from the J, or "Yahwist" source of the Pentateuch.
>
> The Hebrews believed that God revealed the personal name YHWH (probably pronounced as "Yahweh") to Moses. Because of this, the priestly writers (P source) refer to God as Elohim prior to Exodus 6, but include usage of Yahweh afterward.
>
> In the commentary we will refer to the deity as God, Yahweh, or the LORD (all caps is the typical way of showing that the underlying word is Yahweh). In the Hebrew text, however, only the divine epithet "Yahweh" is used in 12:1-9.

God, but we may be confident that God was quite capable of getting Abraham's attention. The story assumes that Yahweh spoke, and Abraham listened. ⚜

God challenged Abram to get out of town. The command had a progressive nature, beginning with instructions to leave his country, with all of its many deities and attendant cultural practices. God then called Abram to leave his kindred, the large tribal unit to which his family belonged. Finally, God told Abram to leave his father's house, the extended family that came with them to Haran.

We can't help but notice that God called Abram to leave behind all that was familiar to him, but without telling him where he was to go: "Go from your country and your kindred and your father's house to the land that I will show you," God said. That Abram responded obediently to such an ambiguous call is testimony to tremendous trust. It is no wonder we look to Abram as a model of faith (see Heb. 11:8-16).

> **For Reflection:** *Put yourself in Abraham's sandals. If God came to you with a similar call, how would you respond? What would it take to convince you that it was really God?*

RADICAL PROMISES
(v. 2)

God's challenging call was accompanied by equally impressive promises. First, God promised to show Abram a new land. That promise implied continued protection and guidance along the way. Abram was assured that God would travel with him, and would speak again.

God offered further promises that were more explicit and remarkable. Keep in mind that the story claims God was talking to a 75-year-old man with no

⛏ **A great name:** The narrator's emphasis on God's promise to give Abraham a great name may be a purposeful contrast to the preceding chapter, in which the builders of the tower of Babel set out to "make a name for ourselves" (11:4). The builders of Babel had everything going for them: countless people, adequate resources, and impressive technical skills. Yet, their prideful effort resulted in a scattering of their people and a loss of their name.

Abram had little with which to build, but the Lord promised to make for him a great name. Through the years, countless generations have looked up to "Father Abraham" as the progenitor of Israel and a model of faith.

children, yet promised "I will make of you a great nation, and I will bless you, and make your name great, so that you will be a blessing" (v. 2). The reader already knows that Abram's wife Sarai was barren (11:30), so this seems to be an unlikely promise. A great nation requires a great number of people. How could Abram become a great nation when having children seemed out of the question?

Yahweh also promised to bless Abram with a great name. In years to come, countless generations would remember his name, and praise it. ⛏

For Reflection: *Names are important. Some people are ambitious enough to hope for such fame that they have a "great name," but that won't happen for most of us. Whether we are remembered by many or by few, we will be remembered. When people recall your name, what will they think? What would you like them to think?*

A RADICAL BLESSING
(v. 3)

God intended not only to bless Abram, but also to make him a blessing to others (v. 2). This thought is expanded in v. 3: "I will bless those who bless you, and the one who curses you I will curse; and in you all the families of the earth shall be blessed."

Did you get that? Abram would become a channel of blessing to all the families of the earth. What an amazing promise! It was not an unconditional promise, but a potential one. Those who recognized Abram as the servant of God and the source of blessing would experience blessings through him. In contrast, those who opposed Abram would also be opposing the work of God, and they would experience a less desirable outcome. ⛏

In time, that stream of blessing would become evident in many ways. The story says that Lot, Abraham's nephew, was richly blessed through their association.

⬇ **Be blessed, or bless themselves?** Some versions of the Bible translate the last phrase of v. 3 as "by you all the families of the earth shall bless themselves" (RSV). This is possible because the niphal form of the Hebrew verb can be translated in a passive or reflexive sense as context demands. This context clearly favors the idea that Abram would become a source of blessing to all persons.

Laban (a descendant of those who remained in Haran) later profited through his affiliation with Jacob, Abraham's grandson. This blessing was not limited to other family members. The Egyptian official Potiphar prospered from his association with Joseph, Abraham's great-grandson. Much later, prophetic hopes centered on a day when all nations would come to Jerusalem to seek God's wisdom and blessings (Isa. 2:2-4). Christians believe the greatest blessing the world could ever receive is Jesus Christ, who was a descendant of Abraham as well as David.

For Reflection: *The Apostle Paul interpreted the life and work of Christ as the ultimate fulfillment of God's promise to make Abraham a blessing to all people (Gal. 3:6-14). How does God continue to bless others today? Could it be that the spiritual descendants of Abraham are still involved?*

RADICAL OBEDIENCE
(vv. 4-9)

The remainder of our text provides a very brief overview of Abram's journey from Haran to the promised land. The long and difficult expedition is passed over in a single clause ("When they had come to the land of Canaan. . .", v. 5b). At Shechem, in the heart of the land, Yahweh appeared to Abram again and confirmed that he had arrived in the land of promise, and the promise was still good: "To your offspring I will give this land" (v. 7a). Abram built an altar there to commemorate the event, then moved on to Bethel, where he built another altar (v. 8). Building altars was not only an act of worship, but also a way of remembering God's promise and claiming the land.

The narrator closes this section with an intriguing observation: "And Abram journeyed on by stages toward the Negeb" (v. 9). The Negeb (sometimes spelled "Negev") was the large area comprising the southern part of Canaan. Though desert-like now, it was a populous place of pastures and small cities during the Middle Bronze Age, the era of the patriarchs. It was a most suitable place to provide pasture for Abram's considerable flocks, and so it became his home.

For Reflection: *Abram moved by stages toward the Negeb. How can this observation serve as a helpful metaphor for our own journey toward spiritual maturity and the experience of God's blessings?*

Abraham's story challenges us to believe that God calls ordinary people to follow him, even when they don't know where they are going, and God's blessing to them becomes a blessing to others.

God doesn't go looking for just the smartest people, the best-looking people, the most talented people, or the richest people. The only thing unusual about Abram and Sarah is that they were in their 70s and had no children, and that's really not the kind of qualification most of us would look for if we were on the search committee for the father of a new nation. In fact, we'd scratch him off the list completely. But God didn't, because God could see what was really important: Abraham's willingness to trust and obey, even when he didn't know what was next.

God calls ordinary people to follow him, even when they don't know where they are going. God didn't say, "Abraham, I want you to go to the land of Canaan, and it is a beautiful green land where the sheep grow fat and the water runs clean and the wheat grows tall." No, God didn't tell Abraham anything about where he was going. Just, "Go to a land that I will show you." It could have been the wilderness of Moab or the deepest jungle in Ethiopia or the hot desert wasteland below the Dead Sea. It could have been anywhere. Abraham didn't know where he was going; he just believed that he could trust God to keep his promises. As it turned out, Abraham ended up going to a lot of different places.

> ⬆ Enter salvation: Gerhard von Rad, one of the most eminent Old Testament scholars of the 20th century, saw God's blessing of Abraham as the birth of salvation into history:
>
> "The promise given to Abraham has significance, however, far beyond Abraham and his seed. God now brings salvation and judgment into history, and man's judgment and salvation will be determined by the attitude he adopts toward the work which God intends to do in history."[1]
>
> In von Rad's view, the blessing was not so much through the promises to Abraham, but through the new channel of response to the God who promises.

God calls ordinary people to follow him, even when they don't know where they are going, and God's blessing to us becomes a blessing to others. This seems a most unusual thing, but it is really a most wonderful thing: God not only promised to bless Abraham, but he also promised to make Abraham's life a blessing to other people.

Can we believe that God still calls to ordinary people like you and me? In the Bible, we have access to more revelation about God than Abraham knew. Unlike Abraham, we have heard the good news that God's call and God's blessings through Jesus extend even beyond this life and into eternity. So, we know more than Abraham did about our ultimate destination—we know a little more about what is at the end of the road—but we don't know all the places that road will go in between.

Those of us who are all grown up can think back to the day we finished high school or the day we left our parents' home and try to remember what we thought we would be doing with our lives, and compare that to where we are now. I doubt many of us knew then where we would be now.

Life is like that. We get to make decisions about where we will go and what we will do, but we never know what will happen when we get there, and how God may have been involved in bringing us to where we are. The important thing is not so much where we go or whether we can claim that God led us every step of the way, but whether we seek to be obedient wherever we are, whatever we are doing.

THE HARDEST QUESTION
How would Dr. Seuss explain this text?

I confess that this question has probably never occurred to anyone but me, but in reading this text about God's challenge and Abraham's willingness to set out for a place unknown, I couldn't help but recall a challenging children's book by Theodor Geisel, better known as Dr. Seuss. In *Oh, the Places You'll Go*, he challenges children to look forward to what's coming. He says:

> You have brains in your head. You have feet in your shoes.
> You can steer yourself any direction you choose.
>
> You're on your own. And you know what you know.
> And YOU are the guy who'll decide where to go.
>
> You'll look up and down streets. Look 'em over with care.
> About some you will say, "I don't choose to go there."
> With your head full of brains and your shoes full of feet,
> you're too smart to go down any not-so-good street.
>
> And you may not find any you'll want to go down.
> In that case, of course, you'll head straight out of town.
> It's opener there in the wide-open air.

Out there things can happen and frequently do
to people as brainy and footsy as you.

And when things start to happen don't worry. Don't stew.
Just go right along. You'll start happening, too.

Seuss goes on to describe the high times and the low times of life, the busy times and the lonely times, and the certain times and the mixed-up times. But he concludes that there are good things ahead for each of us, and he expresses confidence that we all have the ability to go where we need to go and do what we need to do to find a life of blessing.

For believers, the important thing is not so much where we go, but who we take with us. Are we aware that God's Spirit dwells in us, that God can be at work in us and through us wherever we are?

When we think of God's call to us, of three things we may be certain:

1. We will never know in advance all the places our journey may lead or all the people God will bring into our lives.
2. As we follow faithfully, God will bless us with fulfillment and joy.
3. God's blessing to us will become a blessing to others.

God wants to be at work in ordinary people such as you and me. Whether you are blessed with cheerfulness or with riches or with talent or with organizational ability or with a love for children, if you choose to be at home with God, God can take that same blessing that enriches your life and use it to enrich others.

Life is always open-ended for those who seek God's way—always open to new possibilities, to new ways of being blessed, to new ways of blessing others, to new ways of moving mountains if necessary to make this world a better place. So ...

be your name Buxbaum or Bixby or Bray
or Mordecai Ali Van Allen O'Shea,
God calls you to follow, God calls you today!
Your homeland is waiting. So get on your way![2]

NOTES

[1]Gerhard von Rad, *Genesis: A Commentary, Old Testament Library* (Westminster/John Knox Press, 1973), 160.

[2]Quotations from Dr. Seuss, *Oh, The Places You'll Go* (Random House, 1990). The last bit of verse is my own.

Genesis 17:1-22

PROMISES, PROMISES

No longer shall your name be Abram,
but your name shall be Abraham;
for I have made you the ancestor of a multitude of nations.
—Genesis 17:5

Try to remember a time when you were promised something, but had to wait for it. Were you promised a new bike for Christmas? The privilege of dating when you turned 16? The gift of a car when you graduated from high school?

Perhaps you had to wait for weeks, or months. Can you imagine waiting 25 years for a promise to be fulfilled? To hold on to the hope of a promise-come-true, you would probably require periodic assurances from the one who made the promise.

This is precisely where we find old Abram as we read Genesis 17. God had made promises to him many years before, and the would-be patriarch had been waiting for a long time.

A BIG BACK STORY ...

The story claims that Abram was 99 years old when this story took place. 99! He was old, but he was active. Abram had moved from his home in Mesopotamia on the strength of God's promise to bless him with a family to follow him and a land in which they could live. He was already 75 when he made that move: three-quarters of a century in the rearview mirror and starting over (Gen. 12:1-4).

Abram's wife Sarai was 65 at the time, but still considered to be so beautiful that Egypt's pharaoh wanted her for his harem (Gen. 12:10-20) when the couple had gone to Egypt during a time of famine. It is an unseemly story, as Abram had tried to pass Sarai as his sister for fear that the Egyptians would kill him for his wife. The pharaoh took Sarai into his home for some time and didn't return her until Yahweh afflicted Egypt with plagues—a foreshadowing of the Exodus stories to come later.

Incredibly, a story in Genesis 20 claims that the same thing happened many years later, when Abram had become Abraham and Sarai was renamed Sarah. If the chronology could be believed, Sarah would have been around 90 when the king of Gerar was also so struck by her beauty that he took her into his harem after Abraham again tried to save himself by claiming she was his sister.

But we digress. When they returned from Egypt after the famine, Abram and Sarai found Canaan to be accommodating. They enjoyed the land God had promised, but had no luck with the second part of the promise. Children were not forthcoming, though the text records several additional accounts of God's promise to that end.

As noted previously, evidence suggests that multiple writers contributed to the narratives in Genesis, and one bit of evidence is that God's promise to Abraham is repeated several times. The initial story of call and promise (12:1-3) comes from an author known as the Yahwist (abbreviated as J). "J" is probably the oldest layer of tradition, and refers to God by the name "Yahweh." Both J and the Priestly writer (P) include restatements of the promise that Abram and Sarai would have children.

The Yahwist repeats the promise three times, at 13:14-16, 15:1-6, and 18:1-15. We'll look more closely at ch. 18 further on in the book. The second promise occurs after the story about Abraham and his nephew Lot being so prosperous that the land could not sustain all of their flocks, so they reached an amicable separation and Lot moved toward the "cities of the plain," where he took up residence in the city of Sodom despite its notorious reputation (13:1-13).

Perhaps Abram was concerned about his household being divided with Lot's departure when the voice of Yahweh came to Abram, saying, "Look from the place where you stand to the north, south, east, and west. I will give all the land that you see to you and your descendants forever. And I will make your descendants like the dust of the earth, so that if anyone is able to count the dust of the earth, then your descendants also can be counted. Get up and walk throughout the land, for I will give it to you" (13:14-16, NET).

The most formal promise in the Yahwistic source follows the story in Genesis 14 of how Lot and the people of Sodom and Gomorrah were captured by a coalition of five local "kings," whose combined forces Abram was able to defeat with a small army of 318 servants. ♦ After setting the captives free and recovering all their goods, Abram was congratulated by a mysterious figure known as Melchizedek, identified as the king of Salem (Jerusalem) and priest of El Elyon (the High God). Abram surprisingly paid tithes to Melchizedek. In time the Hebrews came to believe that El, El Elyon, and Yahweh were one and the same.

⍟ **Kings:** Obviously, the definition of what it takes to be a king has changed through the years. During the Middle Bronze Age, where the stories of Abraham are often located, much of Palestine consisted of small city-states in which the leaders of cities (consisting of less than 1,000 residents) laid claim to surrounding lands and called themselves kings of the resulting "city states."

Winning victories, saving Lot's skin, and being blessed by a priest (14:1-24) should have been rewarding, but must have reminded Abram that he was still childless. As he expressed despair at having no heir, Yahweh appeared in a vision, led Abram outside, and said, "Look toward heaven and count the stars, if you are able to count them . . . So shall your descendants be" (15:4-5).

Despite the odds, the story says, Abram "believed the LORD; and the LORD reckoned it to him as righteousness" (15:6), an observation that would later become important to New Testament writers. ⍟

⍟ **Faith and righteousness:** Both the apostle Paul and Martin Luther would later put much emphasis on Gen. 15:6—"And he believed the LORD; and the LORD reckoned it to him as righteousness"—in support of their belief in justification by faith. Paul based his argument in Romans 4 on the understanding that God's covenant with Abraham was based on a promise, and all Abraham had to do was believe it.

The promise was followed by a formal (and spooky) covenant ceremony in which Yahweh instructed Abraham to cut up several animals and put their parts in two rows. This was apparently a common practice for formal covenant ceremonies: the two parties making an agreement would walk between the animal halves as a way of agreeing that they might also be cut in two if they broke the covenant. The Hebrew expression for covenant making, in fact, is "to cut a covenant."

This covenant was different. As Abram fell into a deep sleep, "a deep and terrifying darkness descended on him." Yahweh promised again that Abram would have a natural heir, whose descendants would become aliens in another land for 400 years, but come out with great possessions (another foreshadowing of the Exodus). Yahweh then caused a "smoking fire pot and a flaming torch" to pass between the animal parts, thus sealing the covenant along with yet another promise that Abram's descendants would possess the land currently inhabited by others (15:7-21).

Chapter 16 relates the familiar account of how Sarai gave up on the promise and persuaded Abram to impregnate the Egyptian maid Hagar so she could give birth as a surrogate mother, and Sarai could claim the child as her own. Abram cooperated and a son named Ishmael ("God hears") was born, but jealousy erupted between Sarai and Hagar after that, leading to strife and an unhappy situation.

> **For Reflection:** *Has anyone made a promise or pledge to you, but you had so much trouble believing it that he or she found it necessary to repeat the promise often?*

A LASTING COVENANT
(vv. 1-8)

With ch. 17 we come to another covenant promise, this one from the pen of the Priestly writer. The story begins with a note that Abram had reached the age of 99 when Yahweh appeared to him, saying, "I am God Almighty (El Shaddai); walk before me and be blameless" (v. 1). Patriarchal texts in which God appears as the source of life and fertility often use the title El Shaddai, which is typically translated as "God Almighty," though the meaning is uncertain. (See "The Hardest Question" on pp. 19–20 for more.)

As God (known as Yahweh) had called Abram to "go . . . to the land I will show you" (12:1), now God (known as El Shaddai) challenges Abraham to "walk before me and be blameless" (v. 1). The word for "blameless," tamīm, was also used to describe Noah (Gen. 6:9) and Job (1:1, 8), both stellar examples of righteous living.

These, then, were the primary covenant requirements on Abram's part. He was to walk faithfully/blamelessly before God, who pledged to make him "exceedingly numerous" (v. 1b) and "the ancestor of a multitude of nations" (v. 4).

Abram fell on his face at the very thought of a centenarian siring a multitude, but God was serious, announcing that Abram's name would be changed to "Abraham" as a sign of the covenant (v. 5). Both names are dialectical variants of the same word, which means something akin to "Exalted Father." ♲

Further promises in vv. 6-8 reinforce the pledge that Abraham would be "exceedingly fruitful," the ancestor of nations and of kings. God's covenant would last "throughout their generations" as they lived in the land of Canaan, to be given to them "for a perpetual holding."

> ♲ **A new name:** The significance of God's changing the name "Abram" to the longer variant "Abraham" may rely in part on a rhyme found in the Hebrew that English readers do not see: God promised that Abraham (pronounced "*av-raham*") would become the father of a multitude ("*av-hamōn*"). Every use of the name *Av-raham* would bring an echo of the promise that he would be *av-hamōn*, the father of a multitude.

A CUTTING REQUIREMENT
(vv. 9-14)

The Priestly source is marked by a particular interest in cultic and ritual require-ments, so it comes as no surprise that this story adds the stipulation that male circumcision would become a mark of Abraham's and his descendants' identity "throughout their generations" (vv. 9-10).

Circumcision was defined as the cutting of "the flesh of your foreskins"—the prepuce covering the head of the penis. For Abraham and his household, it was to be done immediately, as a sign of the covenant (v. 11). Then, as new boys were born into the clan, circumcision was to take place when they were eight days old (v. 12).

Note that the rule of circumcision did not apply to Abraham and his descen-dants alone, but also to the relatives and servants who made up his extended household—at least 318 adult males, according to Gen. 14:14. One did not have to be a literal descendant of Abraham to be counted among those living in covenant with God as Hebrews (vv. 13-14).

The practice of circumcision was neither new nor unique to Abraham's descendants. Other cultures, including the Egyptians, had practiced it long before Abraham, though not necessarily requiring it of every male. In their cultures, it may bcen used to mark priests or government officials. ♆

After Israel's settlement of the land, and particularly in the post-exilic period, circumcision was strongly emphasized as a mark of Hebrew identity. "The uncir-cumcised" were regarded as heathens, and any Hebrew male who wasn't circumcised was to be "be cut off from his people" for breaking the covenant (v. 14). Highlighting the covenant sign of circumcision and believing it went back to Abraham would have been especially appealing during that period, where the Priestly writers are usually located.

Many years later Paul cited this very story when arguing that faith, rather than circumcision, was the key to living in covenant with God. Paul held that Abraham had believed the promise and had been reckoned as righteous (15:4-6) for years before he was told to practice circumcision

♆ **Circumcision:** Evidence of circumcision among the Egyptians includes rather graphic wall reliefs in the tomb of Ankhmahon, a court official under Pharaoh Teti (c. 2345 BCE), in the city of Saqqara. It was not universally practiced, but probably common among certain types of priests or royal officials. We should not be troubled that circum-cision, thought to be so distinctive of the Hebrews, did not originate with them. As Terrence Fretheim puts it, God took an existing practice and "baptized it" for use in the commu-nity of faith.[1]

(17:9-14)—that is, long before he could be identified as a Jew. Thus, Paul insisted, those who argued that Christian males must be circumcised failed to understand the difference between faith and works.

For Reflection: *What is the most solemn oath or covenant in which you have taken part? A marriage ceremony? Signing the mortgage papers when buying a house? How does it feel to make a long-term commitment?*

A NEW GENERATION
(vv. 15-22)

As Abraham received a new name, so Sarai's name was changed to Sarah, a less archaic form of the same name, which means "Princess" (v. 15). If Abraham was to be the father of kings, it was appropriate that their mother be a princess: "I will bless her, and moreover I will give you a son by her," God said, repeating the promise that nations and kings would rise from her offspring (v. 16).

Though v. 3 had Abraham falling to his face in worship, he responded to God's latter promise with a different kind of fall. He "fell on his face and laughed" at the thought: "Can a child be born to a man who is a hundred years old? Can Sarah, who is ninety years old, bear a child?" (v. 17).

Finding the promise hard to believe, Abraham spoke up for Ishmael, his son by the maid Hagar: "O that Ishmael might live in your sight!" (v. 18). God, however, insisted that a son would be born to Sarah, and that his name would be Isaac—meaning "he laughs," or "may he laugh" (v. 19).

Given that both Abraham (17:17) and Sarah (18:9-15) laughed at the thought of having a child, the boy's name would be a perpetual reminder of God's faithfulness despite their skeptical responses.

God's covenant with Abraham would pass down through his son Isaac (v. 19, 21), but Ishmael was not forgotten. God promised to make him "the father of twelve princes" and ancestor of "a great nation" (v. 20). A tribe known as the Ishmaelites would later interact with Israel, both peacefully and not. To this day, Arab Muslims trace their ancestry to Abraham through Ishmael, and the rivalry continues.

We may wonder why stories of Israel's covenant with God should be of interest to modern believers, but they remind us of an important truth. God has been at work for a long time. God desires to live in a positive relationship with humans, and is willing to call us time and again. God wishes for us to follow on the right path and experience promised blessings, but we have the option of accepting the promise and being true to it—or choosing to follow our own way.

And that's no laughing matter.

THE HARDEST QUESTION
Why was God also called El Shaddai?

The divine title "El Shaddai" (alternatively spelled "Shadday") appears 48 times in the Old Testament as an alternate name for God, especially during the time of the patriarchs. Exodus 6:3 suggests that this was a primary title during that time, before the name Yahweh was revealed. There God explained to Moses "I appeared to Abraham, Isaac, and Jacob as God Almighty (El Shaddai), but by my name 'The LORD' (Yahweh) I did not make myself known to them." Today's text is consistent with this, as God said to Abraham "I am God Almighty (El Shaddai); walk before me, and be blameless" (Gen. 17:1).

The word "El" is a generic term meaning "god," one that could be used with reference to the gods of other peoples. The Hebrews adopted a plural form of the word, "Elohim" (translated as "God") to distinguish the God of Israel above all others. Grammarians call it a "plural of majesty."

"El" appears as a prefix in several alternate titles for God: Melchizedek was a priest of "El Elyon," typically translated as "God Most High" (Gen. 14:18-20). Hagar called God "El Roi" (Gen. 16:13), which means "God Who Sees."

El Shaddai is commonly translated as "God Almighty," though its original meaning is uncertain. The Hebrew word *shad* is used to describe the female breast, with the dual form being *shaddayim*. This suggests that "El Shaddai" carries an image of divine motherhood or giver of fertility, which would be appropriate in this setting as it promises children to both Abram and Sarai. El Shaddai is also used in other contexts related to God as a giver of fertility, and Gen. 49:25 specifically speaks of Shaddai as one who gives "blessings of the breast and the womb."

Some scholars lean toward the translation "God of the Mountain(s)," based on cognate evidence from neighboring cultures. In the Akkadian language, which the Hebrews would have encountered in Babylon, the word *shadu* means "mountain." Since isolated mountains may have a similar profile to a female breast, the Hebrew cognate *shad* may be related.

Some gods were thought to rule from mountains. For example, the Canaanite god El ruled from Mount Zaphon; and similar terminology was sometimes echoed in the assertion that Yahweh ruled from Mount Zion (Pss. 9:11, 20:2, 48:2, 76:2, 84:7, 99:2, and others). Some Akkadian texts speak of gods as "big mountains" (*shadu rabu*), and a similar word was used for a god in a text found at Deir 'Allah, in northern Jordan.

Some scholars have suggested that *shaddai* is a variant form of the verb *shadad*, which means "to destroy," with a first-person pronominal suffix. "God of My Destruction" and even "God, My Destroyer," however, seem unlikely titles for a deity who promises to make Abraham the father of many nations. Other commentators have argued that the word carries a sense of self-sufficiency, so that El Shaddai is the "all-sufficient one."

Most modern translations render El Shaddai as "God Almighty," mainly because Jerome used the word *omnipotens* in his 4th century CE Latin translation that became known as the Vulgate. The Vulgate was the dominant translation for more than 1,000 years, and had much influence on the King James Version of the Bible.

When El Shaddai appears in Genesis, it is nearly always in the context of God as the source of life and fertility (Gen. 17:1-8, 28:3, 29:31, 30:22-24, 35:16-18, 35:11, 43:14, 48:3, 49:25).

The name also appears outside of Genesis, usually as "Shaddai" alone. It is a primary name for God in Job, where it occurs 31 times, and is also used by Balaam (Num. 24:4, 16), Naomi (Ruth 1:20-21), Isaiah (Isa. 13:6), Ezekiel (Ezek. 1:24, 10:5), and in the Psalms (Pss. 68:14, 91:1). In these contexts, the title typically views God as the sovereign king of the world who either blesses and protects or brings curses and judgment.

In our text for today, El Shaddai appears in the context of promising that Sarah will have a child, consistent with its common usage in Genesis.[2]

NOTES

[1]Terrence Fretheim, "Genesis," in *The New Interpreter's Bible*, vol. 1 (Abingdon, 1994), 460.

[2]While much of this explanation is drawn from a variety of Bible dictionaries, the latter part leans heavily on footnote 3 to Gen. 17:1 in the NET Bible, 1st ed. The notes were edited by W. Hall Harris, et al. (Biblical Studies Press, 2005).

Genesis 18:1-15

NOT DEAD YET

So Sarah laughed to herself, saying,
"After I have grown old, and my husband is old,
shall I have pleasure?"
—Genesis 18:12

Have you ever gotten news that seemed too good to be true—news so good that you could only laugh in disbelief? Maybe you won a big prize, or were selected for an honor, or received an unexpected promotion or raise. Maybe someone gave you an extravagant gift, or you learned that your first grandchild was on the way.

Today's lesson tells the story of a couple easily old enough to have great-great-grandchildren being told that they would soon conceive their first child. No wonder they laughed. I suspect we would have giggled, too.

AN ABANDONED HOPE

Genesis 18 is part of the extended story of Abraham and Sarah, which begins in the latter part of Gen. 11:26 and extends through Gen. 25:11. After growing up as Abram in the Sumerian city of Ur (near modern Basra, Iraq), Abraham migrated northward around the Fertile Crescent with his father and extended family. Their initial goal was Canaan, but they stopped and settled in the city of Haran, in northern Assyria (now near the border between Syria and Turkey).

Abraham presumably followed the family practice of worshiping the moon god, but after Abraham's father died, Yahweh appeared to Abraham in some unmistakable fashion, calling him to follow the true God and leave Haran for a new place to be revealed on the way. The call was accompanied by an expansive promise that the LORD would bless Abraham and make of him a great nation, blessing others through him (12:1-3). Abraham was already 75 years old, but pulled up stakes and followed God's call.

God led Abraham to the land that would later become Israel, repeating or expanding the promises at several points along the way. In 13:14-18, God promised to make Abraham's offspring like the dust of the earth, and to grant them "the length and breadth of the land" for them to live on. This made it clear that the promise involved both progeny and property.

Despite God's promise, years passed with no babies in sight. In time, Abraham despaired of having children and prepared to designate Eliezer, his steward, as his heir (15:1-3). Yahweh appeared again to assure Abraham that he would have a child of his own, then led him outside. "Look toward heaven and count the stars, if you are able to count them," Yahweh said. "So shall your descendants be" (15:4-5).

That promise was followed by a hair-raising night-time ritual of covenant making. God instructed Abraham to cut in half a heifer, a nanny goat, and a ram (all three years old), placing the halves across from each other, along with a dove on one side and a pigeon on the other, with a path between them. As evening approached, Abraham fell asleep, "and a deep and terrifying darkness descended upon him." Yahweh again insisted that Abraham's descendants would inherit the land, and Abraham watched as "a smoking fire pot and a flaming torch" passed between the two rows of animal parts to seal the covenant. ⬇

> ⬇ **Covenant, or promise?** The eerie ceremony of Gen. 15:7-20 reflects an ancient tradition of "cutting a covenant," in which two parties making a covenant would apparently kill and divide an animal, then walk together between the pieces as a way of acknowledging they might be cut in half if they didn't keep their end of the bargain (Jer. 34:18).
>
> In this story, however, two symbols of God's presence passed between the carcass parts as Abraham watched. This indicates that the ceremony served more as a solemn promise from God to Abraham than a formal covenant between two parties.

Still another promise is found in 17:1-22, where God changed Abram's name to Abraham and Sarai's to Sarah (both are dialectical variants of the same names, which mean "Exalted Father" and "Princess"). Speaking to Abraham, God promised specifically that Sarah would have a child—after which Abraham could have texted "ROTFL." Modern folk who use text-speak aren't really "Rolling On The Floor Laughing," but Abraham was: "Then Abraham fell on his face and laughed, and said to himself, 'Can a child be born to a man who is a hundred years old? Can Sarah, who is ninety years old, bear a child?'" (17:17).

While Abraham was laughing, God was serious, and this promise contained a new stipulation that Abraham must obey. He was to begin the practice of

> ♆ **Why so many stories?** The several repetitions of God's promise to Abraham emphasize the promise, but also reflect multiple streams of tradition that the author wanted to preserve.
>
> Stories of the promise in Genesis 12, 13, 15, and 18 derive from what critical scholars call the "Yahwist" source (J). Note that in each of them, God is referred to as "LORD," indicating the name "Yahweh."
>
> The promise account in ch. 17 comes from a different source known as the Priestly writer (P), who preferred to call God "Elohim" or "Shaddai" prior to the revelation of God's name as Yahweh in Exodus 3. In that account, then, the deity is called "God," the typical translation of Elohim. The Priestly writer was also particularly concerned with ritual matters such as circumcision, which he said God commanded in conjunction with the promise (17:9-14).

circumcision and require his children to maintain the custom throughout all generations (17:9-14). ♆

> **For Reflection:** *If you received news as shocking or preposterous as the promise that Abraham and Sarah would have a child in their old age, how might you announce the news in a phone text or on Facebook?*

A HOSPITABLE MAN
(vv. 1-8)

When we come to Gen. 18:1-15, God's promise of progeny is repeated, but this time in a more personal manner. Abraham had been in the land for more than 20 years. Some years before, at Sarah's urging, Abraham had fathered a son by Hagar, his wife's handmaid (16:1-16). He seemed satisfied enough for Ishmael to be his heir (17:18), but God had other plans.

The story tells us that Abraham was encamped at a favorite spot called "the oaks of Mamre," which was near Hebron, in a hilly area west of the Dead Sea. As he sat napping in the doorway of his tent in the heat of a dry afternoon, the old man looked up to find three men standing nearby.

The reader knows that Yahweh has come to pay Abraham a personal visit ("The LORD appeared to Abraham by the oaks of Mamre," v. 1), but Abraham does not know his visitors are divine. The trio must have been impressive in appearance, however, for Abraham quickly hustled out to meet the men, bowed with his face to the ground, and begged them to rest in the shade and take refreshments before passing on, "since you have come to your servant" (vv. 1-5).

⯆ **Setting the stage:** We don't know at what point Abraham recognized his guests as none less than God and two angels, but his over-the-top show of hospitality began before he understood who the visitors were, and set the stage for the contrasting inhospitable behavior shown by the people of Sodom in the story that follows (18:16–19:29).

While readers often assume that Sodom and Gomorrah were destroyed because of homosexuality, the narrative's clear point is that the people were wicked and inhospitable. The practice of male-on-male rape as an act of shaming has been common throughout history. Sodom was not a city of homosexuals, but of cruel and unwelcoming people who wanted to shame the visitors through public rape. A similar story occurs in Judg. 19:22-26.

Later biblical references to Sodom make it clear that the crime of the Sodomites was their hostile rather than hospitable behavior toward strangers. Ezekiel, for example, criticized faithless Israelites as being like "your sister Sodom" because they had an excess of food but would not share it with the poor and needy (Ezek. 16:49-50, compare Isa. 3:5-12).

Hospitality was, and remains, an honored custom among Middle Eastern peoples. Even enemies could receive hospitality and protection if they sought it. We are not surprised, then, that Abraham received his visitors with warmth and generosity, but the text describes a particularly extravagant display. Though pushing 100 years old, Abraham ran to meet the visitors, hurried to ask Sarah to bake bread, and again ran to the herd to select a choice calf. He then organized a lavish and hefty meal with dishes of fresh bread, beef, milk, and curds (a form of yogurt). Treating the visitors as honored guests, he "stood by them under the tree while they ate" (v. 8). ⯆

For Reflection: *How would you respond if three uninvited guests suddenly showed up at your home? Modern Western customs of hospitality are less extravagant than those of the East, and hungry or homeless people are unlikely to come knocking at our doors. Are there ways we can still show hospitality to people in need? Should we?*

A WONDERFUL PROMISE
(vv. 9-15)

At some point during or after the meal, the visitors asked "Where is your wife, Sarah?" (v. 9). Had Abraham told them his wife's name, or was their knowledge of her name the first clear indication of their supernatural identity? Abraham answered that Sarah had remained in the tent. This is not surprising. Sarah wasn't hiding or showing pique: it was customary in that culture for men to eat apart from the women, and for the women to remain out of sight.

One of the guests—presumably Yahweh—then declared: "I will surely return to you in due season, and your wife Sarah shall have a son" (v. 10). If Abraham had not yet guessed that his visitors were not ordinary people, that statement should have made it clear.

Sarah's tent was close enough for her to overhear the conversation. At 90 years old and long past menopause (v. 11), she had lost any hope of bearing children, but not her sense of humor: "So Sarah laughed to herself, saying, 'After I have grown old, and my husband is old, shall I have pleasure?'" (v. 12). It wasn't just the idea of children she found hard to believe: the thought of enjoying pleasurable sex with Abraham in their old age must have seemed ludicrous.

The notion was not at all absurd in Yahweh's book, however. "The LORD said to Abraham, 'Why did Sarah laugh, and say, "Shall I indeed bear a child, now that I am old?" Is anything too wonderful for the LORD? At the set time I will return to you, in due season, and Sarah shall have a son'" (vv. 13-14). ♥

In the Hebrew, Yahweh's response comes across as incredulous that Sarah should have doubts. A more literal translation would be: "Why, this? Sarah laughed, saying . . ." Yahweh's description of Sarah's statement is more detailed and emphatic than previously reported. The narrator had mentioned only Sarah's soft laughter at

> ♥ **At what time?** God's promise in v. 10 is especially emphatic, using a special Hebrew construction that combines two forms of the verb. The literal rendering, "returning, I will return," would be understood as "I will surely return."
>
> But when would God return?
>
> The phrase translated "at the set time" could mean "according to the time of life" or "time of living," or perhaps "time of her life." Some take "living" in the sense of "reviving," as the land does in spring, and see it as an indication that Isaac would be born the next spring. If interpreted as "time of her life/ living," it might be a reference to the completion of Sarah's pregnancy. The term is used only here in vv. 10 and 14, and in 2 Kgs. 4:16-17, all in the context of a predicted birth.

the thought of sexual pleasure, but God has Sarah saying: "Indeed, truly, will I bear a child when I am old?"

Yahweh went on to ask, "Is anything too wonderful for the LORD?" The word translated as "wonderful" (NRSV) comes from a verb that can mean "to be extraordinary" or "to be amazing." Since extraordinary things are not easy to accomplish, it can also mean "to be difficult." Thus, NET has "Is anything impossible for the LORD?" and NIV 11 has "Is anything too hard for the LORD?" This is probably the better sense in this context.

The answer to the question, of course, is "No." Nothing is too wonderful, too marvelous, too difficult for the LORD—even the gift of a child to a 90-year-old woman and her centenarian husband.

Fearing that God might be angered by her doubt, Sarah denied having laughed (v. 15). Yahweh did not criticize Sarah or condemn her disbelief. We can almost imagine the "man" through whom Yahweh appeared chuckling as he responded, "Oh yes, you did laugh."

As it turned out, Sarah did indeed have pleasure as well as a son (21:1-7), and laughter was again the order of the day. Abraham had laughed out loud at the news, and Sarah had laughed more quietly, but when the boy was born, they happily named him "Isaac" (*Yitzhak*), which means "he laughs."

"God has brought laughter for me," Sarah said. "Everyone who hears will laugh with me." Today we may still laugh at the prospect of God granting a baby to an aged woman, but Christian descendants of Abraham can rejoice even more in remembering how God, in due season, granted another baby—to a virgin.

> **For Reflection:** *Have you ever heard such unexpected or happy news that you could only respond with laughter and disbelief?*

THE HARDEST QUESTION
How did Abraham realize he was entertaining angels—and God?

The story is carefully told so that the reader will know who is visiting Abraham before Abraham does: "The LORD appeared to Abraham by the oaks of Mamre, as he sat at the entrance of his tent in the heat of the day" (v. 1).

Some effort is given to describing Abraham's gradual realization that someone was there. The Hebrew says "he lifted his eyes and looked, and behold, three men were standing across from him" (v. 2). The preposition I've translated as "across" can mean "against," "on," or "over," but the guests clearly weren't looming over Abraham. The text suggests that the strangers were standing nearby, but at a respectful distance, waiting to see how they would be received. After all, Abraham had to run to meet them.

Abraham's quick and extravagant response may lead one to think that Abraham immediately recognized them as supernatural, but it is more likely that he thought they were people of some nobility who were passing by. The previous stories suggest that God had spoken to Abraham several times before, but none suggested that Yahweh had appeared in human form.

One of the strangers must have been more impressive than the other two and was presumably the leader, for Abraham addressed only him: "My lord, if I find favor with you, do not pass by your servant" (v. 3). He asked the trio to stop, rest, and take a meal, but added "after that you may pass on" (vv. 4-5). This suggests that Abraham still thought of them as travelers passing by his tent. He did not yet understand who they were or that they had come to bring him a message before going on to Sodom and Gomorrah.

Abraham remained respectful throughout the meal as he would have if the guests had been human nobility. There is no indication that he thought of them as supernatural; if so, he would probably have been scraping and bowing rather than standing beside them beneath the tree.

Although it is possible that the guests would have questioned Abraham about his family during the meal, the story suggests that the question "Where is your wife, Sarah?" came out of the blue (v. 9). The men's knowledge that Abraham's wife was still living—and named Sarah—may have been Abraham's first clear hint that his guests were more than human.

The lead speaker's confident insistence that he would return, and that Sarah would give birth to a child, was an added indicator that the stranger was a human-like manifestation of Yahweh. Further evidence of divine knowledge follows Sarah's response. The text says that when Sarah overheard Yahweh's promise, she "laughed to herself, saying ..." (v. 12). Yet, though Sarah had laughed silently and spoken only within herself, Yahweh knew how she had responded: "What's this? Why did Sarah laugh and say ...?" (v. 13).

If Abraham still had questions about his guests' identity, they would have been answered when Yahweh said "Is anything too wonderful for the LORD?" (v. 14). Sarah, too, must have realized the speaker's identity, for she "denied, saying 'I did not laugh'; for she was afraid." Sarah feared, but Yahweh had the last word: "No, but you did laugh" (v. 15).

When the guests prepared to move on and Abraham walked with them, there was no doubt that he was bargaining for Lot's life with no one less than Yahweh.

Genesis 21:8-21

NO LONGER ALONE

Come, lift up the boy and hold him fast with your hand,
for I will make a great nation of him.
—Genesis 21:18

Have you ever faced a major setback that led to a surprising leap forward? Sometimes we complain that our progress in life feels like "three steps forward and two steps back," or even worse, "two steps forward and three steps back."

Still, an apparent obstacle or reversal may turn into an unexpected advantage. Some of the most successful entrepreneurs crash and burn in their early ventures, but learn from failure to create a better product or a more effective business model. Any number of people have been rejected or discarded by someone they had expected to love for life, but kept going forward and found greater happiness, whether alone or with a new and better matched partner.

Today's text describes a mother and son who were cast from a comfortable camp into a desert wasteland. On the verge of losing all hope, they discovered that they were not alone, and could anticipate an impressive future.

THE UNCHOSEN

While the main focus of the "patriarchal narratives" is on the descendants of Abraham chosen to become the ancestors of Israel, considerable attention is also given to the unchosen. The rise of the Hebrews is accompanied by a series of sidetrack stories in which the narrator insists that many of the enemies who would cause the Israelites such trouble in the coming years were also their cousins, descended from unchosen members of the family.

Let's drop back to chapter 13, and Abraham's nephew, Lot. When their joint flocks became so large that there was conflict between their shepherds as well as the local Canaanites, Abraham suggested that they split up, and Lot chose to settle in a fertile area near the cities of Sodom and Gommorah. In doing so, the narrator seems to suggest that Lot chose to leave behind the promise and the Promised Land (13:1-12).

Later, in the aftermath of Sodom's destruction and the death of Lot's wife (reportedly turned into a pillar of salt for disobeying the command not to look back, 19:1-26), Lot was afraid to live in a city, so he took his two unmarried daughters into the hills, where they lived in self-imposed exile. In time, the daughters despaired of finding husbands there but still wanted children, so they conspired to get their father drunk two nights in a row, and took turns having sex with him.

Both daughters got pregnant. The firstborn gave birth to a son who was given the name Moab, and the second had a boy that she named Ben-'Ammi. With no further detail, the narrator tells us that Moab became the father of the Moabites, and Ben-'Ammi gave rise to the Ammonites (19:37-38). The lands of Moab and Ammon were east of the Jordan and the Dead Sea. They and the Israelites would become bitter enemies, but they were not the only ones. ♙

> ♙ **Names:** The Hebrew writer probably intended for the names given to the boys born to Lot and his daughters to be disparaging. "Moab" sounds like a Hebrew phrase that could mean "from father," and "Ben-'Ammi" means "son of my people."

There were other rivals, too. Abraham's son Isaac, born to his wife Sarah, was chosen over his son Ishmael, born to Sarah's handmaid. Before we come back to that story, we note that Isaac and his wife Rebekah had twin sons. The story portrays Jacob as the one chosen to carry on as leader of Abraham's descendants, but reminds us that Esau does not disappear.

Esau married at least three Canaanite women and possibly more—the traditions are mixed and a bit contradictory (28:6-9, 36:1-43). The end result is that Esau's children reportedly became the progenitors of the Edomites. The narrator wants there to be no mistake about the origin of the Edomites. He tells us no less than five times that "Esau is Edom" (25:30; 36:1, 8, 19, 43), and devotes the whole of ch. 36 to their genealogy and Edom's history. The Edomites lived south of the Dead Sea, and became some of Israel's bitterest enemies. The Book of Obadiah, among other texts, is a screed against the hated Edomites and their perceived crimes against Israel.

These descendants are not alone. At some point (not necessarily after Sarah died), the text says that Abraham had married a woman named Keturah. She bore him six sons, one of whom was named Midian (25:1-6). He became known as the progenitor of the Midianites, who appear to be closely associated with the Ishmaelites, who caused Israel much grief before being defeated by Gideon (Judges 6–7).

And where did the Ishmaelites come from? That's the subject of our current study.

For Reflection: *Have you ever felt pressure from family members, school-mates, or the community to be "the chosen one," expected to accomplish great things? Or, have you felt decidedly unchosen while others appeared to be favored? How does it feel to be in either position?*

TROUBLE IN THE CAMP
(vv. 8-13)

We are familiar with the story (Gen. 18:1-15) of how God and two angels visited Abraham's camp near Hebron and told him that despite their old age (100 and 90), he and Sarah would soon have a natural-born son. They both laughed at such a preposterous idea, but in the face of all odds, Sarah gave birth to a boy. They named him Isaac, meaning "he laughed."

Sarah's good humor did not last, however. We recall that some years before, Sarah had given up on bearing a child of her own and decided to use her Egyptian handmaid as a surrogate birth-mother. She encouraged Abraham to inseminate Hagar, the plan was successful, and Hagar became pregnant (16:1-3). Unfortunately, Hagar then "looked with contempt on her mistress" (16:4) and Sarah responded in kind, treating Hagar so harshly that the slave girl ran away (16:5-6).

Through a beautiful but often-overlooked encounter between Hagar and the "angel of the LORD," God not only provided for Hagar's needs in the wilderness, but also promised that her son—to be named "Ishmael"—would grow into a "wild ass of a man" and become the progenitor of uncounted offspring, though he would live at odds with his kindred (16:7-12). 🔵

🔵 **Hearing and seeing:** Both hearing and seeing are important images in Gen. 16:7-14. Before the child was born, God told Hagar to name him "Ishmael," adding, "for the LORD has given heed to your affliction" (16:11). In Hebrew, Ishmael is *yishma'el*, which means "God heard," or "God heeded." A literal reading could be "you shall call him 'God heard,' because Yahweh has heard your affliction."

The image of sight comes from Hagar's response. Hagar is the only person in scripture credited with giving God a new name. "You are El-roi," she said, which means "God of seeing" (16:13). Hagar was amazed that she had seen the angel of the LORD (often an expression describing the appearance of God in human form) and lived, for it was commonly believed that no one could see God and live (a belief echoed in Gen. 32:30 and Exod. 33:20).

⚓ **Playing, or mocking?**
While we might like to think that Ishmael doted on his younger brother and enjoyed playing with him, the story is told from Sarah's perspective, and she clearly saw Ishmael's behavior in a negative light. The only other times the same word is used without modifiers are Exod. 32:6 and Judg. 16:25, both implying negative behavior.

In the first case, the rebellious Israelites made a golden calf and then started to "play," or "revel." In the second, the Philistines called for the blinded Samson to "play for" or entertain them.

Two other instances, where the verb is used with an adverbial phrase, were used by Potiphar's wife to wrongly accuse Joseph of mocking them by assaulting her (Gen. 39:14, 17). Another usage, which describes an adult Isaac as playing with or "fondling" his wife, is more neutral, though seen with disapproval by King Abimelech (Gen. 26:8).

Whether Ishmael was innocently laughing with Isaac, or derisively laughing at him, we cannot know. In either case, Sarah found it offensive enough to demand that Ishmael and his mother be sent away.

God instructed Hagar to return to Sarah with a more respectful attitude (16:9), and the text implies that she did. We read nothing more of their relationship for more than a decade, until the day when Abraham and Sarah held a feast to celebrate Isaac's weaning. In those days, lacking the baby foods and nutritional supplements of today's diet, children were typically weaned near their third birthday.

The happy celebration turned sour when Sarah noticed Ishmael, who would have been 17 or 18 years old if we take the text's chronology seriously. Something about Ishmael and what he was doing offended Sarah, but we can't be sure what it was. A literal reading of v. 9 could be "Then Sarah saw the son of Hagar the Egyptian, which she had borne to Abraham, playing." The interpretive problem lies in our understanding of the last word, which is a participle formed from the same verb meaning "to laugh" that was the basis of Isaac's name.

The participle is formed from an intensive stem, which can give it nuances ranging from "he laughed" to "he played" to "he mocked," in the sense of laughing derisively. The NRSV assumes that Ishmael was innocent of ill will, translating the verse to say that Sarah saw Ishmael "playing with her son Isaac" (the phrase "with her son Isaac" is not in the Hebrew text, but is reflected in the Septuagint, an early Greek translation).

Some other translations choose the more critical shading of the verb to cast Ishmael's behavior in a negative light. The NET, for example, has: "Sarah noticed the son of Hagar the Egyptian—the son whom she had borne to Abraham—mocking" (see also NIV 11 and NAS 95). ⚓

Whatever brought Ishmael to Sarah's attention, she apparently could not bear the thought of Hagar's son being on a par with Isaac. Not even dignifying them with names, she insisted that Abraham "cast out this slave woman with her son, for the son of this slave woman shall not inherit along with my son Isaac" (v. 10). Her demand "was very distressing for Abraham on account of his son" (v. 11). We can imagine what a hard place this created for Abraham, who loved his son Ishmael and did not share Sarah's insecure jealousy, but who still loved and wanted to please his wife.

We wonder if Abraham prayed about it. Though he was torn, the narrator says God told Abraham to accede to Sarah's wishes and send them away, promising that Ishmael would become the father of a nation of his own, while the people to be known as Abraham's descendants would be descended from Isaac, the chosen son of Abraham and Sarah together (vv. 12-13).

> **For Reflection:** *Have you ever been in a position like Abraham, caught between a rock and a hard place? How did you decide what to do? Was prayer involved?*

DELIVERANCE IN THE DESERT
(vv. 14-21)

So once again, Abraham obeyed his wife, sending Hagar and Ishmael into the wilderness with nothing more than a small supply of bread and water. A tanned goatskin water bag could hold 2-3 gallons, but that wouldn't last long in a dry wilderness. They went miles to the south "and wandered about in the wilderness of Beersheba," apparently lost. It would not have taken many days for both food and water to run out, and soon Hagar despaired for their lives. The narrator does not record any speech from Ishmael, though he later says that "God heard the voice of the boy." ✡

Ishmael would have been in his late teens, according to the canonical chronology, but the story speaks as if he were much younger, using a term typically employed for a small child. After their scant provisions were exhausted and thirst had taken its toll, Hagar "cast the child" under a bush and then went "about the distance of a bowshot" away, believing the boy would die soon and not wanting to watch (v. 15-16).

Hagar "lifted up her voice and wept," the text says (v. 16), and we assume Ishmael must have been crying, too, for comfort arrived when "God heard the voice of the boy." In response, "the angel of God called to Hagar from heaven, and said to her, 'What troubles you, Hagar? Do not be afraid, for God has heard the voice of the boy where he is'" (v. 17). Though Hagar had hidden her son beneath the bush, he was not hidden from God. ✡

⚓ **How old was Ishmael?** Gen. 21:9-19 portrays Ishmael as a young boy, old enough to walk but still being held by the hand. The canonical chronology suggests that he could have been as old as 18, however:

- He was 13 when Abraham circumcised him (17:25).
- Abraham was 75 when he left Haran (12:4) and had been in the land for 10 years when Sarah suggested that he get Hagar pregnant (16:3), which would make him 86 when Ishmael was born (see 16:16).
- Abraham was 100 when Isaac was born (21:5), so Ishmael was about 14 at the time.
- The feast Abraham threw to celebrate Isaac's weaning would have been about three years later, making Ishmael about 17, and quite old enough to carry the water that Abraham reportedly put on his mother's shoulder.

While the disparity may be due to differing source materials, perhaps it is best to imagine that the narrator, in focusing on the desperate circumstances of Hagar and her son, considered that the story would be more poignant if Ishmael was portrayed as a much younger child.

⚓ **Dumping the boy:** The NRSV's translation "she cast the child under one of the bushes" gives the impression that Hagar tossed a small child she had been carrying into the shrubs. The verb is used only in the causative stem, and usually means something akin to "throw" or "fling." It's the same word used to indicate that Joseph's brothers threw him into a pit (Gen. 37:20, 22, 24), that the Israelites threw down the king of Ai's body by the city gate (Josh. 8:29), and that priests threw Jeremiah into a cistern (Jer. 38:6, 9). In this sense, we might also use the word "dumped."

Ishmael would have been too big to fling away from Hagar, but we have the impression that the boy, having grown weak, may have been leaning on her for support, and she dropped him in the shadow of a bush.

The angel instructed Hagar to help the boy up and lead him by the hand, "for I will make a great nation of him" (v. 18). He then "opened her eyes" to a nearby well, from which she could refill the water skin and revive the boy (v. 19).

Both God and Hagar looked after Ishmael as he grew, according to v. 20: "God was with the boy, and he grew up; he lived in the wilderness, and became an expert with the bow." While they lived in the wilderness of Paran, south of the Negev and close to Egypt, Hagar arranged a marriage for him with an Egyptian woman (v. 21)—and that's the last we hear of Hagar.

It's also the last we hear from Sarah. Surprised?

For Reflection: *It's hard to imagine how it would feel to be in Hagar's sandals, torn between her love for Ishmael and the pain of seeing him suffer. In a similar situation, how do you think you would respond?*

A TALE OF TWO MOTHERS

We would not expect Sarah to appear in the following chapter, the story of how Abraham came close to offering Isaac as a burnt sacrifice. If she had known what Abraham was up to, it would surely have been the death of her. Indeed, ch. 23 begins with Sarah's death in Hebron and the account of how Abraham purchased a burial cave for her—but much time had passed, for Isaac was then 40 years old.

Take note of the ambivalent way the narrator portrays Sarah: he admires her beauty and her willingness to play along with Abraham's tricks. But, he also sees Sarah as the first to give up on the promise of descendants by resorting to surrogate motherhood rather than trusting God to grant her a child. Given Sarah's age, we can understand that, but in the narrator's mind, this puts Sarah in a negative light, a shadow that emerges more strongly when Sarah begins to resent the results of her own plan and turns against both Ishmael and her handmaid, who had obediently allowed Abraham to impregnate her.

But the narrator also shows mixed feelings about Hagar. She obeys her mistress and accepts her role as a surrogate mother, but adopts a spiteful attitude toward Sarah after becoming pregnant. When treated harshly, she runs away, only to return and bear the child, then be forced to leave the camp with no more thanks than a loaf of bread and a skin of water. In the wilderness, she dumps Ishmael under a bush and retreats, leaving him to die alone rather than staying to comfort him in what she expected would be his last moments.

Despite Hagar's weak moments, she is granted two conversations with God. In the first encounter, God speaks to her and she speaks to God. Indeed, she assigns to God a new name—*El Roi*—and is the only person in scripture said to have done so (16:13). In the second encounter, Hagar does not speak, but God provides water and again promises that her offspring—like Abraham's—will multiply beyond counting.

While biblical tradition asserts that the Israelites were descendants of Abraham through Isaac and then his son Jacob's 12 sons, it likewise assigns to Ishmael 12 sons who became progenitors of their own tribes, and who interfaced with their Israelite cousins in ways both positive and negative. As Jews look to "Father Abraham," Muslims of Middle Eastern descent also consider Abraham to be their ancestor, but through his firstborn son, Ishmael. Given the current tension many people feel toward those who follow Islam, it is good to remember that they also call Abraham father.

THE HARDEST QUESTION
Why did Paul call Hagar the mother of Israel?

Although their stories are told in Genesis, both Sarah and Hagar reappear in the interpretive tradition of scripture, and in curious ways. Sarah is named in the company of Abraham in Isa. 51:2 as the mother of Israel's faith. Similarly, we assume that Isaiah had Sarah in mind when he spoke of the barren mother who would give birth to many (Isa. 54:1-3).

Sarah and Hagar also appear in the New Testament, where Paul treats them in surprising fashion. In an argument for salvation by faith, Paul twists the Genesis traditions with a bold metaphor that aligns Hagar with Mount Sinai and the law, giving birth to children who were destined to slavery. In Paul's metaphor, which quotes from Isa. 54:1, he sees Jews who are enslaved to the law as descendants of Hagar, while Christian believers, like Isaac, are descendants of Sarah and the true "children of the promise" (Gal. 4:24-31).

This is doubly interesting, because in the Genesis tradition, Hagar serves as a counterpoint to the notion that God's care was limited to the chosen people of Israel. Hagar's only narrated conversations are with the same God Abraham served, and that same God made promises to Hagar not unlike those made to Abraham.

Walter Breuggemann has pointed out that Hagar "functions in the narrative to keep the horizon of Israel open to 'the other' who also has legitimate claims to make upon the promise of God."[1]

So, while in Genesis Hagar is a reminder of God's persistent care for the "unchosen" and Sarah is the mother of the Israelites. Paul chose to reverse the two, portraying the slave woman Hagar as the spiritual mother of Jews who were enslaved to the law, while depicting Sarah as the mother of Christians who trust God by faith and become "true children of the promise."

NOTE

[1] Walter Breuggemann, *Introduction to the Old Testament: The Canon and Christian Imagination* (Westminster/John Knox Press, 2003), 50.

Genesis 22:1-14

THE CLOSEST CALL

"He said, "Do not lay your hand on the boy or do anything to him;
for now I know that you fear God,
since you have not withheld your son,
your only son, from me."
—Genesis 22:12

Can you imagine being asked to stand in Abraham's sandals—to bind your only child, lay him on an altar, slice his throat, and light a fire beneath him? The thought is horrifying beyond measure. Yet, the Bible insists that God asked Abraham to do that very thing—as a test—to determine if he was truly faithful and worthy of the blessing God had already promised several times before. ♦

As it has come down to us, the story is both warmly touching and deeply troubling. It speaks of confident faith on the part of Abraham and Isaac: Abraham trusts God, and Isaac trusts Abraham. Yet, such testing seems abusive. Would God command a father who had waited 100 years for a son to take that beloved child and return him to God as a burnt sacrifice? ♦

While modern readers can certainly debate whether they believe God would have asked such a thing, the biblical writer had no doubt, and we must deal with the story from his perspective. Note how the writer masterfully evokes deep

♦ **The source of the story:** Scholars often note that Genesis 22 is one of the most carefully crafted stories in the Old Testament. The story refers to God as Elohim (mostly, but not always), and is often labeled as an E, or Elohistic story. The simple, bare bones telling of the story, however, smacks of the Yahwist source. The story uses Yahweh as a name for God in vv. 11, 14, 15, and 16. Some scholars have suggested that the story was very old, perhaps first written by the Yahwist, then later edited by the Elohist.

⊎ **Genesis 22 and the Broadman Bible Commentary:** Back in the 1960s, the Southern Baptist Convention's Sunday School Board prepared to publish a Bible commentary, in which British Baptist G. Henton Davies wrote the commentary on Genesis. Davies did not believe God would have put Abraham through such a terrorizing trial, and offered a psychological argument that Abraham, aware that some of his pagan neighbors occasionally sacrificed their children, had convinced himself that God had called him to do the same thing.

When the commentary was published in 1969, it stirred such controversy that messengers to the next Southern Baptist Convention demanded that the Sunday School Board recall the commentary and assign it to a new writer. A revised volume was published in 1973, written by Clyde Francisco of Southern Baptist Theological Seminary.

Francisco allowed that Abraham may well have asked himself whether he loved his god as much as some of his pagan neighbors loved theirs, but insisted that "It was not a test that Abraham gave himself ... a man so signally led and blessed by God would have had to hear from God himself the actual imperative to make the sacrifice" (pp. 187-188).

Today, copies of the Broadman Commentary's original volume one are considered collectors' items.

emotion without using a single word of feeling. He never speaks of fear, or pain, or heartache, or conflicting emotions—and yet the artful and often repetitive arrangement of actions and words grabs the reader's heart, and squeezes. (A rather literal translation of the story can be found at the end of the chapter, following "The Hardest Question.")

In reading the story, we recall that in the previous chapter, Abraham had lost his son Ishmael after giving in to Sarah's demand that he and his mother be sent away. God had promised to make a great nation out of Ishmael even though he would not be the ancestor of the promised people. Would God also find a way to keep the promise alive if Abraham obeyed his command to sacrifice Isaac?

We also recognize that the story of call and promise in Genesis 12 is in the background of this story. Abraham's obedience to God's initial call cut him off from his past; if he obeys this new command, it will cut him off from his future. Yet, the story portrays Abraham as incredibly trusting, apparently confident that the God who had worked miracles in his life before could still do wondrous things, could still fulfill the promises and covenant he had made time and again.

For Reflection: *Thinking of Jesus as God's son, some have observed that readers should remember that God did not ask Abraham to do something God was not also willing to do. Does that thought make you feel any better about this story?*

A TERRIFYING TEST
(vv. 1-8)

The story begins with a terrifying demand. The narrator knows it is a test, and the reader knows (v. 1), but Abraham knows only that God has told him to "Take your son, your only son Isaac, whom you love, and go to the land of Moriah, and offer him there as a burnt offering on the mountain that I shall show you" (v. 2).

How could Abraham not protest? Why is there no questioning? Could anyone truly trust God so ardently that he or she would slaughter a child with no word of complaint?

The author presents Abraham as an icon of trustfulness, so any recriminations or self-doubts he might have entertained remain hovering in the background. This engages the reader more deeply. We must imagine what was going on in Abraham's mind and heart and belly as he got up early the next morning, chopped wood for the sacrificial pyre, bound it onto his donkey, and gathered his son and two servants to begin a long journey fraught with uncertainty (v. 3).

Sarah does not appear in this story, though she had a prominent role in the previous chapter. The future lies in Abraham's hands alone. Will he follow through? If he does, what will happen to the promise? Will Sarah, past 110 years old, have yet another child?

The narrator relates the long walk in dreamlike silence. No words were spoken until the third day, when Abraham saw the mountain ahead, and told the servants to stay with the donkey while "the boy and I will go over there; we will worship, and then we will come back to you" (v. 5). Is Abraham so trustful that he believes God will somehow let him escape the wrenching task ahead, or is he soft-peddling misdirection so the servants remain ignorant of his plans? Surely they, like Isaac, would have known that everything needed was present except the sacrifice.

Tension builds as the author tells how Abraham laid the large bundle of wood on his son's back—indicating that Isaac would have been a young man of some size—while Abraham himself carried a smoldering pot of coals and a sharp knife (v. 6). The implication is that a boy might hurt himself if entrusted with such dangerous items, but both the danger and the items rest with Abraham.

As they walked, Isaac spoke for the first and only time, voicing the long-unspoken question: "Father! . . . The fire and the wood are here, but where is the lamb for a burnt offering?" (v. 7).

⬇ **Was Abraham lying?** The author of Hebrews believed that Abraham planned to sacrifice Isaac, but expected him to be resurrected (Heb. 11:17-19). In this way, one could explain Abraham's words to the servants as fully truthful.

Again, we do not know if Abraham's reply reveals exorbitant trust or careful dissimulation: "God himself will provide the lamb for the burnt offering, my son" (v. 8). Abraham knew that Isaac was the intended victim, but God had also provided Isaac, so his response could be truthful without being specific. ⬇

For the second time we are told that "the two of them walked on together"—a poignant picture that needs no further description.

For Reflection: *Who do you think exhibits more trust in this story: Abraham or Isaac?*

A TENSION-FILLED CLIMAX
(vv. 9-14)

Once they had arrived at the mountain—traditionally identified as Mount Zion, the future home of Jerusalem and the temple—the narrative moves quickly, as if the author wants to get the scary tension over with. Abraham built an altar, no doubt with Isaac's help in gathering large stones and fitting them into a stable platform. He laid the wood in order to facilitate lighting it on fire at the appropriate time. "He bound his son Isaac"—with no reported resistance or protest from the boy, though it's hard to imagine such a thing could have been done in silence. He then took his beloved son and "laid him on the altar, on top of the wood" (v. 9).

The pivotal moment arrives with v. 10, as "Abraham reached out his hand and took the knife to kill his son." The word for "kill" normally means "slaughter," as in slaughtering an animal by slitting its throat. Can you imagine Isaac lying with throat bared and terror in his eyes? Can you stand with Abraham as he took Isaac's hair in one hand and held the knife poised in the other, trying to work up the nerve to begin the downward slice?

At what point did the angel of Yahweh step in to stop Abraham's hand? Did he wait until Abraham had committed to the stroke, or call out as soon as he raised the knife? We don't know, but our stomachs twist at the thought. Finally, mercifully, God spoke: "Abraham, Abraham!" Feel the hope in Abraham's heart as he replied "Here I am!" (v. 12). ♦

And then there was relief: "Do not lay your hand on the boy or do anything to him; for now I know that you fear God, since you have not withheld your son, your only son, from me" (v. 12).

"Now I know." Did God really need to put Abraham through such a trial in order to know he was faithful? The author does not explain; his purpose is to magnify Abraham's trust rather than to question God's justice. As Abraham had "lifted his eyes and saw" the mountain earlier that day (v. 4), now he "lifted his eyes and saw" a ram in a thicket of brush, held fast by his entangled horns.

Abraham caught the ram and offered it as a sacrifice in place of his son, praising God by calling the place *"Yahweh Yireh,"* usually translated as "the LORD will provide" (v. 14). ♦ We presume that he also loosed Isaac's bindings so he could climb down from the altar. What Isaac thought of the whole scenario is not said.

A RENEWED BLESSING
(vv. 15-19)

With Abraham having passed the test, Yahweh uttered a surprising oath, repeating and expanding on previous promises to make Abraham's offspring as numerous as the stars of heaven and the sand of the seashore, so prosperous that other nations would share in the blessing. ♦

♦ **The angel of Yahweh:** Did an angel call out to Abraham, or was it God? The text speaks of "the angel of Yahweh," but in the Hebrew Bible the expression "angel of Yahweh" implies that God's own self is present through the angelic intermediary. Note that the angel speaks "from heaven" (vv. 11, 14), and clearly speaks for Yahweh: "Now I know . . ." (v. 12), "'By myself I have sworn,' says Yahweh . . ."

The narrator's use of the "angel of Yahweh" assures the reader that Yahweh is present, but provides just enough distance for the recipient of Yahweh's word to avoid having seen God personally—an event commonly thought to have fatal consequences.

♦ **Provide, or see?** Though it can have the sense of "provide" (as in "see to it"), the word *yireh* would normally mean "he sees." The story has been replete with images of seeing, as in the earlier story of God's provision for Hagar, who called God "El-roi," meaning "God who sees" (Gen. 16:13). The same root is used in both cases. *Yireh* is the third-person singular imperfect form of the verb; *roi* is the masculine singular participle.

> ⚓ **A self-directed oath:** Typically, biblical oath-takers swore by their god (or gods), or occasionally by the king—someone who had authority to punish them if they did not fulfill the oath. The standard form, usually much abbreviated in the text, was "May God do so and so to me, if I do not do such and such." The oath was an invitation for God to invoke a penalty if the person did not keep his oath.
>
> God's words were typically considered to have the force of an oath, for there was no higher or more authoritative being to which God could appeal. Thus, Gen. 22:16ff is especially forceful: "'By myself I have sworn,' says Yahweh: 'Because you have done this, and have not withheld your son, your only son, I will indeed bless you ...'"

With no further fanfare or mention of Isaac, the text says Abraham returned to the servants he had left at the foot of the mountain, and they all returned to Abraham's camp in Beer-sheba, and then life went on.

What might this story—and Jesus' story—say to modern believers who seek to please God? Hebrews 2:18, speaking of Jesus, reminds us that "Because he himself was tested by what he suffered, he is able to help those who are being tested." Paul, in writing to the Corinthians, insisted that "God is faithful, and he will not let you be tested beyond your strength, but with the testing he will also provide the way out so that you may be able to endure it" (1 Cor. 10:13).

This dark story may seem troubling, but it is worth the stress it may cause us. It is a masterpiece of literature, written with a simple economy of style that points us inexorably toward one single question: "Could you pass this test? Would you be willing to sacrifice your child for God?"

Before we respond with a blithe, "Of course not," we must ask if the real question is to which God and on what altar will we sacrifice them. Will we ignore our children and sacrifice them to the god of success or business or personal achievement? Will we fail to teach them the importance of love and ethical behavior, thus sacrificing them to the god of selfishness? Will we raise our children without teaching them about the living God of the universe, sacrificing them on the altar of our own faithlessness?

There is a risk involved in teaching our children about the power of God and the love of Jesus. They may take us seriously. They may determine to love other people even when it is difficult, to serve others even when it is dangerous, or to give of themselves in manifold ways for the glory and the love of God. It's a risk we take when we carry them up the mountain of faith and introduce them to the wild and awesome God of Abraham.

Nothing is harder than giving up a child, whether it is giving her up to death or giving him up to a life apart from us. But we can't keep our children forever.

The question is whether we give them up to God, or to the world—whether we are willing to walk with them up the windy mountain of faith, or whether we leave them to find their own way down below.

Abraham's hard choice reminds us of another ugly story in the Bible. On a bleak day in early spring, another young descendant of Abraham climbed his own Moriah. He did not carry firewood on his back, but wood in the form of a cross. No ram would be found in a thicket that day, for he himself was "the lamb of God, who takes away the sins of the world" (John 1:29).

Jesus anticipated a resurrection beyond death, but had to take the risk of trusting God to be true to the promise.

No faith, no ethic, no religion is worth having if it does not ask for sacrifice. Christianity makes no claim to be a religion without cost, a cuddle-blanket designed only to meet the needs of its adherents.

For Reflection: *What are we willing to sacrifice for God?*

THE HARDEST QUESTION
Where was Mount Moriah?

The question of where Mount Moriah was located must also examine whether the term indicated a place name, or means something else.

According to the story, God told Abraham to sacrifice Isaac on "one of the mountains I will show you" somewhere "in the land of Moriah" (v. 2). Verse 3 says Abraham headed toward the mountain God had shown him, and v. 4 says Abraham saw the place, still far away. After God provided a ram as a substitute for Isaac, "Abraham called that place 'The LORD will provide'; as it is said to this day, 'On the mount of the LORD it shall be provided'" (v. 14). "The LORD will provide," in Hebrew, is "Yahweh Yireh," as preserved in some translations ("Jehovah-jireh" in the KJV).

Later Jewish traditions held that a large stone on the Temple Mount was the site of Abraham's sacrifice, further sanctifying the site as appropriate for the temple. Second Chronicles 3:1 tells us that Solomon built the temple "on Mount Moriah," on the former threshing floor of "Ornan the Jebusite," which David had purchased and designated as the temple site.

The image of Moriah as an unsettled mountain but future home of Jerusalem is at odds with an earlier story in which Abraham is said to have paid tithes to Melchizedek, described as the "King of Salem," indicating that Jerusalem was already a walled city.

The Septuagint (an early Greek translation) preserves the name as "*Amoria*," suggesting "in the land of the Amorites." Earlier, Abraham had built an altar at a placed called Moreh, near Shechem (Gen. 12:6). Thus, some scholars believe the place was on a hill near Shechem, which would jive with an early Samaritan belief that the sacrifice took place on Mount Gerizim, which is in that area.

Muslims believe that Ishmael, rather than Isaac, was the intended victim, and identify the place as "Marwah," locating it near the Kaaba, in Mecca, Saudi Arabia.

But it is possible that "Moriah" was not intended as a place name. It is derived from the same verbal root (*ra'ah*) found in references to when Abraham "lifted his eyes and saw," and when he named the place "Yahweh Yireh" (as noted above, *yireh* normally means "to see," but can have the sense of providing, as when we say "I'll see to it").

The Hebrew *moriyeh* can be interpreted as a *hif'il* (causative) participle, meaning "cause to be seen," or "show," which relates to the idea that Abraham would receive a revelation at the place of sacrifice. The Septuagint, an early Greek translation, rendered the phrase as "the land of heights," using a word (*hupselos*) that typically referred to a place above the earth and associated with divine beings. Catholic translations based on the Vulgate call it the "land of visions," rather than "land of Moriah." Possibly seeking to preserve a distinction from the term *moriyeh*, the Hebrew of v. 2 does not conclude with "one of the mountains I shall show you" (as in NRSV), but "one of the mountains that I will tell you."

READ LIKE A HEBREW

Here is my translation of the story, which I have intentionally written in a rather literal way in hopes of preserving some of the Hebrew flavor in the storyteller's art. As you read, take note of what images stand out, either through repetition or by their simplicity.

And it happened, after these things, that God tested Abraham, and he said to him, "Abraham!" and he said, "Here I am."

And (God) said, "Take now your son—your only son—the one you love—Isaac— and go—you—to the land of Moriah, and offer him up as a burnt offering on one of the mountains that I will tell you.

And Abraham rose up early in the morning, and he saddled his donkey, and he took two lads with him—and Isaac, his son. And he cut wood for the burnt offering, And he started out for the place that God told him.

On the third day, Abraham lifted his eyes and saw the place from a distance.

And Abraham said to the lads, "Stay here with the donkey, and I and the boy will go over there: we will worship, and we will return to you."

And Abraham took the wood for the burnt offering and put it on Isaac, his son, and he took in his hand the fire and the knife, and they went on—the two of them—together.

And Isaac spoke to Abraham, his father, and he said "My father!" And he said, "Here I am, my son." And he said, "Look, the fire and the wood, but where is the lamb for the burnt offering?"

And Abraham said, "God will provide for himself the lamb for the burnt offering, my son." And they went on—the two of them—together.

And they came to the place that God told him, and there Abraham built an altar, and he laid out the wood, and he bound Isaac, his son, and he put him on the altar, on top of the wood.

And Abraham stretched out his hand and took the knife to slaughter his son—but an angel of Yahweh called out to him from the heavens and said "Abraham! Abraham!" And he said, "Here I am!"

And he said, "Do not stretch out your hand to the lad, and do not do anything to him, *for now I know that you fear God*, for you did not withhold your son, your only son, from me.

And Abraham lifted his eyes and saw, and look!—a ram—one—was caught in a thicket by its horns. And Abraham went and he took the ram, and he offered it up as a burnt offering instead of his son.

And Abraham called the name of that place "Yahweh Yireh," as it is said today, "On the mountain of Yahweh it will be provided."

And the angel of Yahweh called out to Abraham a second time from the heavens:

"By myself I swear, says Yahweh, that because you have done this thing and did not withhold your son, your only son, that I will surely bless you and I will greatly multiply your descendants like the stars of the heavens or the grains of sand on the seashore, and your descendants will take over the stronghold of their enemies, and by your offspring they shall bless themselves—all the nations of the earth—because you heard my voice."

So Abraham returned to his lads, and they started out together for Beersheba, and Abraham dwelt at Beersheba.

Genesis 24:34-38, 42-49, 58-67

ON THE BRIDAL PATH

Then Isaac brought her into his mother Sarah's tent.
He took Rebekah, and she became his wife; and he loved her.
So Isaac was comforted after his mother's death.
—Genesis 24:67

H ave you ever read a novel or watched a movie that began in the middle
and left you confused? Skillful writers will find ways, as the story moves
along, to fill in the back-story—details that readers or viewers need in
order to understand the actions, motives, or personalities of the characters.

For example, the movie version of *Forrest Gump* opens with a feather gently
riding the soft currents of a warm Savannah breeze, then landing on the foot of a
young man who sits at attention while waiting on a bench at a bus stop. We don't
know who he is, why he is on the bench, or why he speaks so oddly—but we learn
through a series of flashbacks that tell the story of Forrest's life to that point.

Biblical stories also have back-stories that are important if we are to understand the characters involved. Today's text provides the background needed to
appreciate the memorable life of the patriarch Jacob, one of the Bible's most
colorful characters. But it's not about Jacob; it's about his father.

A SERVANT'S MISSION
(vv. 34-38)

Genesis 24 is such a lengthy narrative that we've chosen a few select texts to tell
the story. Verse 34—where the lectionary reading begins when it's the text for the
day—plops us down right in the middle of a story that needs its own back-story.
A servant of Abraham is making a speech before dinner in the home of one of
Abraham's relatives, in the far-off city of Haran. What brought him there?

The story began with Abraham, whom God had called to become the
father of a great nation (12:1-9) at a time when Abraham and his wife Sarah

were childless, old, and unlikely to become parents. After many years and several misadventures, however, they had a son, and they named him Isaac (21:1-7).

Today's story fast-forwards from Isaac's childhood to his mother's death, when Isaac is 40 years old. One gets the impression that he had been a "Mama's boy," because only now does Abraham decide it is time for Isaac to marry. This should catch our attention, because in that culture young men and women typically married in their teens. Abraham had been promised many descendants, but Isaac was old enough to be a young grandfather and still unmarried.

Abraham did not want his son to marry one of the local Canaanite women, but someone from the extended family living back in Haran (11:31). To accomplish this, he sent a trusted servant on the long journey north to find a suitable wife while Isaac remained at home, grieving for his mother. The servant is not named, but usually presumed to be Abraham's steward Eliezer, who would have been Abraham's heir if no children had been born (15:2).

We enter the story after Abraham had assigned his servant the task, swearing him to fidelity through an oath that may have involved touching his genitals, a practice that seems strange to us but may not have been unusual in his day (24:1-9). ♦

The servant loaded 10 camels, according to the story, sufficient to carry supplies for the long journey, along with valuable gifts to serve as a bride price, demonstrating Abraham's wealth and the good prospects a young wife might have in the south.

> **For Reflection:** *While the image of a long camel train is appealing, we should note that archaeologists have found no evidence that camels were domesticated before the 10th century BCE, hundreds of years after Abraham's time. Camels would have been in common use by the time this story was written, however, and the narrator would have had no way of knowing that wild camel-taming was a relatively recent accomplishment. Does this apparent anachronism make the lessons inherent in the story any less meaningful?*

♦ **A serious oath:** Abraham's instruction for his servant to "put your hand under my thigh" while swearing an oath of fidelity is attested in other ancient cultures, and is similar to a later oath in which Jacob (then called "Israel") called upon Joseph to swear that he would not bury him in Egypt (47:29).

The implication is that the servant either held or put his hand beside Abraham's genitals, perhaps in recognition of the genitals as the "vehicle of life."[1] The genitals also suggest, in this situation, the importance of fertility and the propagation of the family through Isaac's descendants.[2]

After many days, the servant completed the long journey to Haran without apparent incident. As he neared the city, the story says, he stopped by a well to pray that God would identify the right maiden (24:10-14), who quickly revealed herself by coming to the well and drawing water for the servant and all of his camels—precisely the sign for which he had asked (24:15-21). ♦

The servant rewarded the young woman with an expensive gold nose ring and two heavy gold bracelets before learning that she was Rebekah, the granddaughter of Abraham's brother Nahor, and thus a perfect match for Isaac (12:22-24). When Rebekah invited the servant to lodge at the family compound, he offered a heartfelt prayer of thanksgiving (24:25-28). Once there, he met the woman's brother, Laban, who took careful notice of Rebekah's new jewelry before inviting the servant to dinner (24:29-33). ♦

Today's text picks up here, as dinner is being served, but the servant refuses either to be seated or to eat before announcing his mission. In short order, he described

> ♦ **A foreshadowing of future relations:** The narrator's observation that Laban took notice of the gold ring and bracelets given to Rebekah before he personally unloaded the camels (to examine what else he had brought?) is an early suggestion that he has a greedy and sneaky streak, one that will come full flower in his later interactions with Jacob, who accused him of constantly changing his wages.

> ♦ **Weddings and wells:**
> The story is a variation on a familiar "betrothal type scene" in the Bible, in which a man and a woman meet at a well and a marriage ensues (for example, Jacob and Rachel in Gen. 29:1-14; Moses and Zipporah in Exod. 2:15-22).
>
> When Jesus met the Samaritan woman at the well, the story also has marital overtones, though they related to the woman's multiple previous marriages (John 4:1-26).
>
> In Old Testament betrothal scenes, the man typically has traveled to a far country when he stops for water at a community well, one of the few places where one could conveniently meet marriageable maidens. In the accounts involving Jacob and Moses, the men draw water in a show of chivalry, but in Genesis 24 it is the maiden who draws water for the servant, who had prayed for a sign—that a woman would come and draw water for him.
>
> As Robert Alter notes, "There is surely some intimation in all this of the subsequent course of the marriage of Isaac and Rebekah—he in most respect is the most passive of the patriarchs, she forceful and enterprising."[3]

how Nahor's brother Abraham had amassed great wealth, how Isaac had been born, and how he had been sent to procure a wife for Abraham's heir. The servant explained that Abraham insisted that Isaac's wife should come from his extended family, but tactfully omitted the patriarch's instruction that Isaac himself should under no circumstance travel to Haran (24:6).

For Reflection: *Before sending his servant to find a wife for Isaac, Abraham required him to swear that he would make every effort to fulfill his responsibility. Yet, knowing that success was not guaranteed, Abraham agreed that if the servant failed to find an appropriate wife, so long as he did his best, he would be absolved of his oath. This may offer some comfort for times when we work hard to build up the church, but see little in the way of results. Do you think God is more concerned with the number of our successes, or the measure of our obedience?*

AN ANSWERED PRAYER
(vv. 42-49)

With the back-story in place, the servant related his earlier encounter with Rebekah. He explained to Rebekah's family how he had prayed for God to reveal the chosen woman by means of her willingness to water the camels, how Rebekah had met every requirement, and how he had thanked God for answered prayer.

Without bothering to ask Rebekah what she thought about it, the servant then put the wedding ball in his hosts' court. Would the family agree to a marriage between Rebekah and Isaac, sending their daughter to live in a far-away land?

While Rebekah remained silent, her father Bethuel and brother Laban politely protested that there seemed to be little for them to say about it, since Yahweh's will had been made known in answer to the servant's prayer (vv. 50-51). Pleasantries and nods to God aside, however, Rebekah's family would still have expected the payment of a generous dowry and other gifts of hospitality. The servant did not disappoint them, distributing costly presents to Rebekah and to other family members (v. 53).

For Reflection: *Have you ever prayed for God's guidance? You may not have had an experience quite like that of Abraham's servant, but can you remember a time when you sensed God's leadership? How did you know?*

A MARRIAGE MADE IN HARAN
(vv. 58-67)

Rebekah's family sought to delay her departure for 10 days of feasting and farewells, but when the steward insisted on leaving immediately, Rebekah was finally given a voice in the matter. Her willingness to go (v. 58) is reminiscent of Abraham's readiness to heed God's call and leave his family behind as he followed God's leadership to the land of promise (12:1-9).

Fittingly, Rebekah's family blessed her as she left—a literary pointer to the father's blessing that Rebekah would later help her son Jacob steal from his brother Esau. The blessing itself—a wish for many offspring who would prosper and "gain possession of the gates of their foes"—foreshadowed Israel's efforts to take possession of the "Promised Land" many years later, after the exodus from Egypt.

The long journey south to Abraham's camp in the Negeb is passed over quickly, but the initial meeting between the two lovers-to-be is played out in near cinematic style. From atop her camel, Rebekah saw Isaac at a distance, then slid to the ground and covered her face with a veil, as was the custom before a wedding.

The narrator omitted any mention of a ceremony, however, cutting to a scene in which Isaac "brought her into his mother Sarah's tent" where "He took Rebekah, and she became his wife; and he loved her" (24:67).

There is much to unpack in these few frames of action. The significance of Isaac taking Rebekah to his mother Sarah's tent leads us to wonder if Isaac did not have a tent of his own. More significantly, it suggests that Rebekah has become the new matriarch of the family. Abraham had wed another woman, presumably after Sarah's death (25:1), but his new wife Keturah did not get Sarah's tent. That tent belonged to Rebekah, through whom the promised line would continue.

Although the new union was an arranged marriage, we are told that "Isaac loved her," and was comforted after his mother's death. The text says nothing about whether Rebekah loved Isaac, but her earlier eagerness to get on with the journey suggests that she was a willing partner in the marriage.

The story of Isaac and Rebekah's marriage seems far removed from courtship as known in Western culture, though arranged marriage is still the custom in some Eastern and South Asian cultures.

What might Christians in a modern Western context learn from this account of a strange practice in a strange land?

We first consider how the story fits into the larger context. Genesis 12–50, often called the "Patriarchal History," focuses on themes of divine guidance and human obedience in the lives of the patriarchs, along with God's covenant promise to Abraham that he would become "a great nation" (12:2). Each generation of patriarchs faced tests of faith and had to overcome obstacles before seeing the birth of children: Isaac himself is most famous for having been born, after all hope had failed, to a 100-year-old father and a 90-year-old mother.

For the line to continue and the "nation" to grow, Isaac would also have to marry and have children. The servant's experience of answered prayer is replete with the theme of divine guidance, reminders that God desires to be at work in the lives of those who seek to follow God's way.

By the end of the story, there is no doubt in the reader's mind that Isaac has found the right woman, but a question yet remains: Will she and Isaac have any more success in having children to foster the beginning of a "great nation"?

> **For Reflection:** *Isaac appears as more of a bridge character between Abraham and Jacob than as an individual in his own right. Yet, bridges are important. God used Isaac and Rebekah as links in the generational chain that led to the formation of Israel. Although you may sometimes feel as insignificant as Isaac, do you believe God can do important work through you, too?*

THE HARDEST QUESTION
What's up with Isaac?

Careful readers can't help but note that Isaac, for all the hope placed in him before his birth, is rarely given space in the narrative to exercise his own personality. When Isaac appears in the narrative, he most often appears as Abraham's son or Jacob's father, not as his own man. And, in most stories, Isaac is either passive or befuddled.

Some readers have pointed to evidence in the stories suggesting that Isaac may have had some special challenges, as one might expect of a child born to aging parents with deteriorating DNA.

As a boy of indeterminate age—but old enough to carry a heavy load of firewood—Isaac meekly submitted to his father, allowing Abraham to bind him and stretch him out on a sacrificial altar, saying nothing as Abraham came perilously close to slitting his throat (Genesis 22). Would an ordinary child be so accommodating?

Secondly, though it was customary for young men and women to marry in their teens, Isaac was unmarried and possibly still living in his mother's tent at the age of 40. Did he need special care?

Isaac did not complain when his father arranged his marriage without consulting him, pointedly not allowing him to accompany the servant to Haran (Genesis 24). Did Abraham think him incapable of making the journey?

When the servant arrived with Rebekah, Isaac immediately took Rebekah to his mother's tent, where without ceremony "she became his wife; and he loved her. So Isaac was comforted after his mother's death" (Gen. 24:67). Did he still need someone to take care of him?

In midlife, Isaac appears to take some independent initiative, but several of those accounts, such as trying to pass off his wife as his sister (while publicly fondling her) and arguing over a well, are quite similar to stories attributed to Abraham (Genesis 26).

As an old man, we observe, Isaac appeared clueless as his wife and sons manipulated him for favors (Genesis 27). Was it just blindness that led Isaac to be fooled by the hairy goatskin collar and arm pads Jacob wore in pretending to be his brother Esau?

Whether he suffered from personal challenges or from the storyteller's art, Isaac could be considered the lost patriarch.

NOTES

[1]Terrence Fretheim, "Genesis" in *The New Interpreter's Dictionary of the Bible* (Nashville: Abingdon Press, 1994), 510.

[2]For an extended discussion of this, see D. R. Freedman, "Put Your Hand Under My Thigh— the Patriarchal Oath," *Biblical Archaeology Review* 2 (1976): 2-4, 42.

[3]Robert Alter, *Genesis: Translation and Commentary* (New York: Norton, 1996), 115

Genesis 25:19-34

BIRTH RIGHTS AND WRONGS

Isaac loved Esau, because he was fond of game;
but Rebekah loved Jacob.
—Genesis 25:28

Have you ever seen a rough-looking biker or other person wearing a T-shirt with the slogan "Born to Lose," or heard one of several songs by the same name? Sadly, the fatalistic fear that one might come into the world with the cards stacked against him or her is a fairly common one.

The Book of Genesis contains the story of a man who seemed born to lose. His name was Esau. Esau's brother Jacob, however, could have sewn a patch on his shepherd's robe declaring that he was "Born to Win."

Do either of those life scripts resonate with you? How we think of ourselves in relation to the world—as winners or losers, as competent or hopeless—can have a great impact on whether we find success in life, or whether we surrender to our own script of failure. A look at Jacob and Esau might offer helpful insights as we imagine what yet lies ahead for us.

Jacob and Esau were twins, and Esau was technically the older brother, but his sibling would prove to be the one chosen to carry on. It is Jacob who was given the name "Israel" and became not only the father of 12 sons who became ancestors of the famous 12 tribes of Israel, but also a mirror or memory in which Israel could see itself facing difficult obstacles (some self-inflicted) but yet surviving.

TWO PRAYERS AND AN ORACLE
(vv. 21-23)

Although we know Jacob will emerge as the most significant character, we will offer Isaac the respect of examining the part he plays in the life and shaping of his sons. ♦

⛉ **Framed by losers:** The stories of Abraham conclude with the genealogy of Ishmael (25:12-18), the son who had been born to him by the Egyptian maid Hagar. This genealogy serves as a literary bracket to close one story and mark the beginning of another. The stories of Abraham's son Isaac—which some would see as a subset of a larger Jacob cycle (25:19–36:43)—begin with what appears to be a genealogy of Isaac's descendants ("These are the descendants of Isaac . . ." Gen. 25:19), but it is really an account of the birth of Jacob and Esau, Isaac's only children of which we have any record.

There is good reason to see the larger picture as a Jacob cycle in which the chosen one's story is bracketed by the genealogy of Ishmael (25:12-18) and the genealogy of Esau (36:1-43). Both Ishmael and Esau were the eldest sons of a patriarch, but passed over as leader of the next generation. Terrence Fretheim has noted "This bracketing of the chosen by the non-chosen may be a way in which these groups of people are held together, not least in the service of God's mission of blessing all 'families' (28:14)."[1]

The motif of "the barrenness of the patriarchal wives" is common in Genesis 12–50. God had promised countless progeny to Abraham, but his wife Sarah remained barren for many years. So, we are not surprised to learn that Isaac's beloved wife Rebekah also appeared to be barren (v. 21). This had apparently been the case for 20 years: Isaac is said to have been 40 years old when he married Rebekah (v. 20), but he was 60 when Jacob and Esau were born (v. 26).

Many things had happened in the intervening years—probably including most of what takes place in ch. 26, where children are not mentioned. Ancient Hebrew writers cared far less about putting things in chronological order than modern writers do. Since the most important thing for us to know about Isaac is that he was Jacob's father, this story is told first.

The narratives do not record that Abraham had prayed for Sarah to conceive, though we presume that he did. Stories about Isaac are limited, but the text does tell us that he prayed for an end to Rebekah's barrenness, "and the LORD granted his prayer, and Rebekah conceived" (v. 21). Not only did Rebekah conceive; she conceived twins.

The story tells us that Rebekah also prayed, not in order to get pregnant, but because her pregnancy proved to be exceedingly difficult. The twins reportedly "struggled together" in her womb. Literally, "they crushed each other," a sign of things to come. This made Rebekah so miserable that she prayed and wondered why it had to be that way (v. 22). ⛉

> 🔖 **A miserable pregnancy:** Rebekah may have done more than complain about
> the difficulty of her pregnancy. Translators of the NRSV, relying on the witness
> of an early Syriac version, have her saying, "If it is to be this way, why should I
> live?" The preserved Hebrew text literally says "If it is thus, why am I this (way)?"
> Whether Rebekah considered her situation a matter of life or death is uncertain.

The text tells us that "Rebekah went to inquire of the LORD," using the same sort of language typically employed to describe a visit to a sanctuary or a conversation with a priest in which one would seek a divine oracle.

In Rebekah's day, however, there was no sanctuary or priesthood in service to the God of Abraham, unless we are to presume something established by Melchizedek, who is called "priest of the God Most High" in Gen. 14:18, and to whom Abraham paid tithes (14:20). Melchizedek is not mentioned after that in the patriarchal narratives, however. We have no way of knowing where Rebekah went, how she went about "inquiring of the LORD," or how she received the oracle that we find in v. 23. Whether she consulted a prophet or priest, or received a vision from God, the narrator does not say.

Through the oracle, Rebekah learned the reason for her difficult pregnancy (twins), and received a prophecy of how the brothers' lives would play out. The oracle is cryptic and couched in poetry, as shown below in this rather literal translation, with suggested clarifications for missing words in parentheses:

Two nations (are) in your womb,
And two peoples will be separated from your belly,
And (one) people will be stronger than the (other) people,
And (the) great (older?) will serve (the) small (younger?).

The firstborn son, it seems, was born to lose.

TWO BIRTHS AND A STRUGGLE
(vv. 24-26)

The narrator delights in wordplay while recounting the twins' birth. Esau is described as "red" (*'admoni*), using the same word translated as "Edomite." The land inhabited by the Edomites is characterized by reddish sandstone mountains, scrub, and deserts. Esau is also depicted as "hairy," using a word that sounds like "Seir," an alternate name for the Edomites' homeland. The name "Esau" also draws on some of the same sounds.

Jacob is said to have been born holding on to Esau's heel (*'aqav*). Thus he is called "*Ya'aqov*," which could mean something like "heel-grabber," "supplanter," "grasper," or "overreacher."

Take note that the narrator describes Esau entirely in physical terms. We are told what he looked like (red and hairy), but not what he does. The text is unclear as to whether it was Esau's complexion or his hair that was red, but something about his appearance was apparently remarkable.

In contrast, the narrator describes Jacob only in terms of action. We are told nothing of what he looked like, but only what he was doing: grabbing at Esau's heel, as if he were trying to pull his twin brother back and beat him out of the womb. Jacob's competitive nature is clear from the beginning: he was born to win.

> **For Reflection:** *Have you ever wondered why only one of Isaac's sons was chosen to carry on the family name as ancestor of the Hebrews? If Esau's descendants had also been considered Hebrews, the population of a "great nation" could have arisen much more quickly. Why do you think only Jacob was chosen?*

TWO BOYS AND A BAD DEAL
(vv. 27-34)

The unhappy story of the boys' disparate proclivities and their parents' dysfunctional partiality is familiar to us. Isaac was partial to Esau because he loved to eat wild game, and Esau's nature was the ancient equivalent of a man in camouflage who drives a pickup with a gun rack in the back. Jacob, on the other hand, is pictured as a homebody who stayed closer to the family compound, which pleased his mother. The parents' favoritism is obvious: "Isaac loved Esau, because he was fond of game; but Rebekah loved Jacob" (v. 28).

As Isaac and Rebekah's 20 years of childlessness were telescoped into a single verse, so were the adolescence and growth to manhood of Esau and Jacob. In vv. 25-26, they are born. In v. 27, they "grew up" and became men—men who struggled with each other as they lived out the prediction of the oracle that preceded their birth.

Wordplay is also important in the quaint story of how Jacob persuaded Esau to sell his birthright for a bowl of stew. The story does not identify what Jacob was cooking when Esau came in from the field, only that he "was seething something seethed" (v. 29). Later we learn that it was a stew made with lentils (v. 34).

The words for "cook," "hunter," and "game" in Hebrew have similar sounds, suggesting perhaps that the hunter may fall victim to the cook.

⛏ **More on wordplay:** Curious about the words? In the first bit of word play, the term for "cook" (*zid*) sounds like the word used earlier for both "hunter" and "game" (*tsayid*). This may subtly suggest a relationship between the cook and the hunter.

The second instance comes into play with what Esau said when asking for some of Jacob's cooking. Literally, he said, "Please feed me the red stuff, this red stuff, for I am famished." The word I've translated as "red stuff" is *ha'adom*, which literally means "the red." Without the article *ha-*, the word is identical to the term for Edom. Thus, the narrator adds, "he was called Edom." Esau would later become known as the ancestor of the Edomites.

A second instance of wordplay is Esau's request for the "red stuff" (a literal translation) Jacob was cooking. The word for "red stuff" is the same as the word for Edom. Later in the narrative, Esau will be called as the ancestor of the Edomites. ⛏

Note again how differently the characters are portrayed. Jacob is conniving, clever, and looking toward the future. Esau appears to be so shortsighted and impulsive that he thinks less of his birthright than a bowl of thick lentil soup, thinking he will die if he doesn't eat, so the birthright would be no use to him. Thus, the text says, "he despised his birthright."

For Reflection: *This story might leave us wondering what things we may have "despised" in service of self over God. Are there ways in which we, like Esau, have "despised" our birthrights as children of God, called to live and love in ways that honor God and better the world? Have we let physical desires or appetites eclipse our inclinations to obey God and serve others?*

The reader may wonder whether either Jacob or Esau knew about the oracle Rebekah had reportedly received. Since the prophecy predicted that the older son would serve the younger, would Rebekah have kept that news from her favorite son? Later, we learn, it was not Jacob but his mother who came up with the plan to cheat Esau out of the older son's blessing by substituting a goat for savory venison, dressing Jacob in Esau's smelly clothes, and masking Jacob's smooth skin with scraps of goat hide tied around his neck and arms (27:6-17).

The story leaves us wondering if Jacob was a naturally born swindler (as his birth story implies), or if his personality was shaped by his mother's determination that he fulfill what she believed to be his destiny.

For Reflection: *Although Esau is the one who seemed to care little for his birthright, the narrator shows no empathy for the conniving way in which Jacob obtained it. Are we ever inclined to use shady means to get ahead or take advantage of other people? If our success comes at the cost of cheating another, is it worth it?*

THE HARDEST QUESTION
Why is the lack of children always blamed on the women?

As noted in the lesson, "the barrenness of the patriarchal wives" is a common theme in Genesis. Sarah, Rebekah, Rachel, and Leah all had difficulty conceiving at one time or another. Why do we never hear of the infertility of the patriarchal husbands?

In the modern world, we understand that both men and women can have problems with fertility, but the ancients knew little about the inner workings of reproduction. They did not understand that the woman provides an egg cell to be fertilized by spermatozoa from the man, producing a zygote that grows into an embryo. Instead, they considered the woman's uterus to be little more than a plot for the planting of a male's seed. If she was fertile, the seed would grow and become a child. If not, she would be considered barren, like a saline or rocky field where nothing would grow—the agricultural metaphors are intentional. On the other hand, if a man was capable of ejaculating, it was assumed that he was fertile. Issues of sperm count or motility were not concepts the ancients had imagined.

For the narrators, it was also easier to speak only of the woman as the one who could not bear children, because they believed it was God who controlled whether a woman's womb was "open" or "closed."

In this sense, God plays a curious role in the patriarchal stories, either preventing or allowing pregnancies in order to demonstrate divine faithfulness. In Genesis 17 and 18, Yahweh declared that Sarah would give birth to a child, but waited until she was 90 years old and had twice been taken from Abraham by foreign kings before engineering his birth.

Rebekah went 20 years without getting pregnant until Isaac finally got a prayer answered. Had he prayed before for Rebekah to conceive, or was the story in Gen. 25:20-21 intended to suggest that he had not prayed until then?

While Jacob apparently slept with both of his wives, God saw that Leah was unloved and left Rachel barren but opened Leah's womb, according to Gen. 29:31. But Rachel was Jacob's chosen bride from the beginning, and he continued to love Rachel most despite her inability to bear children. Nevertheless, Rachel, bitter of soul, must have believed Jacob was holding back in some way, for she complained to Jacob that he had given her no children. Angry despite his love for Rachel, he replied "Am I in the place of God, who has withheld from you the fruit of the womb?" (Gen. 30:2).

After the birth of four sons, Leah's fertility was put on hold for a while, and when both Rachel and then Leah promoted their handmaids as surrogate mothers, Jacob sired children by both Bilhah and Zilpah. Later, following an episode in which Leah allowed Rachel to have some mandrakes (thought to aid fertility) that her son Reuben had collected, she bore two more sons, giving God the credit for each one (Gen. 30:14-20). Finally, we are told, "God remembered Rachel, and God heeded her and opened her womb" (Gen. 30:22), leading to the birth of Joseph.

Gerhard von Rad has classically pointed to the "barrenness of the patriarchal wives" as "J's didactic scheme," a repetitive motif showing that Yahweh's promises might be threatened, but God was faithful and could be trusted to overcome all obstacles. While that may be true, there is a tacit acknowledgment that Yahweh could have granted the women children at any time, so we have to acknowledge that God is not only the one who overcomes the problems, but also the one who set up the obstacles to begin with.

Did the narrator think the repetitive issue of childlessness was an ongoing test to see if Abraham's family would remain faithful in the face of adversity? What do you think?

NOTE

[1]Terrence Fretheim, "Genesis," in *The New Interpreter's Dictionary of the Bible* (Abingdon Press, 1994), 518-19.

LESSON 8

Genesis 28:10-19

BLESSINGS IN THE HOUSE OF GOD

Then Jacob woke from his sleep and said,
"Surely the LORD is in this place—and I did not know it!"
—Genesis 28:16

Have you ever wished you could meet God personally—while still on this side of the border between life and death? Have you ever imagined what it would be like to hear God speak a blessing directly to you?

If such a thing should happen, how do you think you would respond? Would you be overcome with shock and awe and unable to speak? Would you simply bow in humble gratitude and offer what thanks your stumbling tongue could utter?

On the other hand, is there any chance you would listen to the offer, then type up a contract and ask God to sign on the dotted line to confirm that the promised blessings would indeed be fulfilled?

That is very close to what Jacob did when God unexpectedly appeared to him in a dream while he was camped at a place called Bethel. Can you imagine?

TWO STORIES

This familiar story follows the memorable account of how Jacob disguised himself as Esau and swindled his brother out of the blessing his blind and aged father Isaac had intended to bestow on the oldest son (27:1-40). Esau was rightfully angry, and plotted to kill his conniving sibling, but Rebekah sent Jacob away before his brother could act. As he traveled northward to seek refuge with his uncle Laban in Haran, Jacob had an unexpected encounter with the divine.

There appear to be two stories in one here, a well-edited composite of the two oldest source documents behind the Pentateuch, usually called "J" and "E."

> ♆ **Story sources:** As noted earlier, the account of Jacob's blessing at Bethel
> appears to be a composite of traditions from two ancient sources. The J source
> is so named because the narrator typically refers to God as "Yahweh," the
> special name by which God was called. It is called "J" rather than "Y" because
> the German scholars who first identified the source spelled Yahweh as "Jahveh."
> The E source is denoted in part by its characteristic use of "Elohim," a plural
> form of the generic Semitic term for "god," as the preferred divine name.

While the older J source tends to speak of Yahweh as appearing physically in the form of a man, the E source imagines God as being more distant, appearing in dreams or through the medium of an angel. In this story, the larger frame of the story appears to be E, which calls God "Elohim" and speaks of a dream sequence in which Jacob is shown a stairway to heaven. Though we often imagine a ladder (as in the song "We Are Climbing Jacob's Ladder"), the word is more suggestive of a broad staircase: angels are both ascending and descending upon it—an unlikely image for a ladder.

In the middle of E's dream sequence, however, we find a more personal theophany (an appearance of God) from the J source, in which Yahweh speaks directly to Jacob.

The editor/narrator managed the transition seamlessly by inserting it at v. 13 and by using a double-duty combination of a preposition that can mean "upon," "by," or "beside," with an attached pronoun that can mean either "he" or "it." Thus, the resulting word could be translated to indicate either that God stood "upon it" (that is, upon the stairway, from the perspective of E's dream sequence) or "by him" (beside Jacob, from the perspective of J's theophany).

Whether standing *on* the stairway or *by* Jacob, Yahweh spoke audibly to Jacob, self-identifying as the God of his grandfather Abraham and his father Isaac. God went on to repeat to Jacob the basic promise of land and offspring that was previously made to Abraham and Isaac, even expanding it with a promise to be with him everywhere he goes, to watch over him, and to return him safely back to his homeland. Yahweh concluded with the ringing affirmation "I will not leave you until I have done what I have promised you" (vv. 13-15).

TWO RESPONSES

When Jacob awoke from the dream, he was convinced that he had stumbled upon the very gateway to heaven. At first he was overcome with awe and immediately marked the spot by taking the stone he had used to bolster his head and standing it on end, then anointing it with oil to sanctify the place as a holy site. Appropriately he called the place "Bethel," a Hebrew term meaning "house (*beth*) of God (*el*)." 🔻

In v. 20, however, Jacob appears less worshipful and more distrustful. Although Yahweh had made a solemn and unconditional promise to bless Jacob, the young traveler responded with a very conditional vow designed to withhold his recognition of Yahweh until all the promises had been fulfilled.

We recall that when Esau agreed to trade his birthright for a bowl of stew (25:29-34), Jacob had sealed the deal by requiring him to swear an oath. Now, before he would fully accept God's offer, Jacob initiated a conditional vow designed to bind God to the previous promises: he wanted God to deliver before agreeing to join his forbears in acknowledging and worshiping Yahweh.

We can't help but notice that Jacob's vow (vv. 20a-22) does not mention the central pledge of land or progeny, but focused on God's promises of personal patronage and divine protection. This seems to underscore Jacob's self-centered nature. Not only did he key in on personal aspects of the promises, but he also intensified them. Unsatisfied with God's general promise to "watch over" him, Jacob asked specifically for food and clothing. Wanting more than a promise that he would return to the land, Jacob asked to be brought back *in peace*.

Though raised in a family of Yahweh worshipers, Jacob held out even his acceptance of Yahweh as God until he saw the promises fulfilled. In this way, the vow also serves as a framing device for much of the narrative that follows. The vow will be mentioned again in 31:13, when God reminds Jacob of it and tells him to return home, and it is not completed until 35:1-7, when Jacob finally returns to Bethel, builds an altar and offers sacrifices after a peaceful reception by his brother Esau.

> 🔻 **From pillow to pillar:** Jacob's act of setting up a stone pillar to mark a sacred spot follows a familiar pattern in the Old Testament, and standing stones are commonly found in archaeological excavations.
>
> Laban would later set up a pillar as a witness to his final parting from Jacob (Gen. 31:51-52). Samuel set up a stone called "Ebenezer" (stone of help) to commemorate God's aid in a victory over the Philistines (1 Sam. 7:12. Later, Absalom set up a pillar as a memorial to himself (2 Sam. 18:18).
>
> Pillars were also commonly associated with the worship of Baal or other foreign gods, however (2 Kgs. 3:2, 10:26-27), so in time the process came to be frowned upon: Deut. 16:22 forbids it.

For Reflection: *We use the word "vow" differently in our day, but we may pray the same kind of prayers. Have you ever prayed that if God would get you out of trouble, or would give you something special, you would perform some act of service or worship in return? How did that work out?*

TWO QUESTIONS

🔱 **Awakening to the presence of God:** Consider Elizabeth Achtemeier's comment on Jacob's surprise visit from God: "Jacob wakes with a shudder, and in shivering awe he comes to the realization that this is none other than the place where heaven and earth meet. This is the gate of heaven. The Lord has invaded my world, he realizes. I am not alone on this journey.

"Somewhere on our journey through life, we all have had a similar experience —that heaven has invaded our ordinary realm, that we are not alone in our world, but that we are accompanied on our pilgrimage by a mysterious presence, whose name is Jesus Christ. Surely if ever heaven descended to this earth, it did so in that man of Nazareth, and now he walks the road with us, as we go on our common journeys."[1]

Chances are that none of us has had an experience like Jacob's. We haven't slept in the wilderness with our head on a rock, or awakened to a vision of God standing beside our bedroll, promising to make us the father of a nation. 🔱

So, why do we bother to study this text? What can we learn from it?

The story reminds us that we never know where we might meet God, or at least, feel an overpowering sense of the divine. There is nothing we can do to reach God, but the Bible insists that God can reach us, that heaven may come down to meet us in the midst of our need and our fear and our running away.

Jacob learned that he could run from his brother, but he could not run from God. God came to Jacob in the middle of nowhere, bringing surprising words of grace and promise and a future. Even when Jacob responded with a guarded vow that showed his own lack of trust, God did not give up on him, and neither does God give up on us.

As we walk our common journeys, as we run from our fears, as we pursue our dreams, God comes to us. Sometimes, when we *least* expect it, God comes to us in the form of a person or a dream or a sudden conviction or even a sermon that touches the heart. When God comes, we may not respond with great maturity or faith—we may try to work the same kind of distrustful deal with God that Jacob did—but God accepts what trust we have, and continues to work with us and lead us to other times when we may meet God again and grow in our devotion.

A second thing to observe is that the text virtually shouts of blessing. Jacob had done nothing to deserve God's beneficence. Indeed, one would think that his conniving ways would have earned some sort of divine retribution. But, the story suggests that it was in God's mind to bless Jacob as the chosen one to become the head of a new nation. Although Jacob had to leave home and would gain wealth through his wits rather than an inheritance from Isaac, he was blessed in many ways.

We should note that Esau was also blessed. Although he did not receive his father's official blessing to the firstborn, with Jacob's departure he inherited everything. This ultimately gave to Esau even more property than he would have if the estate had been divided the normal way, with the older son getting twice the share of the younger.

Esau's behavior was no more commendable than Jacob's. He was roundly criticized for marrying two Hittite women who made life bitter for Isaac and Rebekah (26:34-35). Yet, he was also blessed.

For Reflection: *Can you think of ways in which God has blessed you, even though you can also think of ways in which you have fallen short of God's purposes for you?*

THE HARDEST QUESTION
Why was Jacob's "vow" so conditional?

In Western culture, we tend to think of vows as unconditional promises such as monastic vows or wedding vows. In ancient Near Eastern literature, however, the term we translate as "vow" always refers to a conditional promise. The biblical narratives contain five examples of such vows, which typically begin with a request ("Oh God, if you will do such and such for me . . ."), followed by a promise ("Then I will do such and such for you . . .").

Jacob's vow (Gen. 28:20-22) is the earliest biblical example. Following the exodus, while traveling through the wilderness, the Israelites corporately pledged to devote everything to God and take no plunder if Yahweh gave them victory over the Canaanite king of Arad (Num. 21:1-3).

During the period of the judges, Jephthah offered a misguided vow, pledging to sacrifice whatever came first from his house if God gave him victory in battle with the Ammonites. Unfortunately, his daughter became the unintended victim (Judg. 11:30-31).

Closer to the period of the monarchy, Hannah, desperate for a child, promised that if God would give her a son, she would return him to God (1 Sam. 1:11).

Later, Absalom claimed to have made a vow to worship God in Hebron if God returned him safely to Jerusalem (2 Sam. 15:8). The vow was a specious excuse for leaving town, since he was preparing to lead a coup against his father, but David could not deny him the opportunity to fulfill the vow (see detailed rules for vow-making in Num. 30:1-16).

The Book of Psalms also contains vows, though the poetic form often obscures the psalmists' promise to praise God when their prayers are answered. Worshipers often prayed for help, and promised to praise God in return (examples can be found in Psalms 22, 54, 56, 59, 61, 69, 109, and others.)[2]

NOTES

[1]Elizabeth Achtemeir, *Preaching from the Old Testament* (Westminster/John Knox, 1989), 65.

[2]For more on biblical vows, see my articles, "Vow," in *International Standard Bible Encyclopedia* (Grand Rapids: Eerdmanns, 1988), 4:998.999; and "Conditional Vows in the Psalms of Lament: A New Approach to an Old Problem," in Ken Hoglund et al, eds., *The Listening Heart: Essays in Psalms and Wisdom in Honor of Roland E. Murphy, O. Carm.* (Sheffield, England: JSOT Press, 1987), 7794; or my book, *Vows in the Old Testament and the Ancient Near East* (Sheffield: JSOT Press, 1992).

Genesis 29:1-30

JACOB MEETS HIS MATCH

Jacob loved Rachel; so he said,
"I will serve you seven years for your younger daughter Rachel."
—Genesis 29:18

Have you ever unwrapped a gift, hoping it was something you wanted? Perhaps the size and weight were right for that blue sweater you'd been hinting about, or a new cordless screwdriver. With keen anticipation, you worked through the wrapping paper, only to discover that the blue sweater was a pink housecoat, or that the cordless screwdriver was a book.

It can be hard to hide our disappointment when reality turns out to be quite different from our expectations, and life surprises us. Try to imagine, though, the astonishment on Jacob's face when he awoke on the morning after his wedding night to discover that his new bride—veiled the night before—was not the woman he expected.

AN AUSPICIOUS ARRIVAL
(vv. 1-14)

The back-story of this intriguing text is Jacob's arrival in the north Mesopotamian city of Haran, where he had come for two purposes: (1) to get far away from his brother Esau, who had threatened murder after Jacob swindled him out of his father's blessing; and (2) to find a bride from the extended family, as opposed to the local Canaanite/Hittite women that Esau had married. ♉

Upon his arrival in Haran, Jacob quickly proved himself a force to be reckoned with. The narrator passes over the journey from Bethel (see the previous chapter) to Haran in short order, but slows down with Jacob's approach to the city. On the outskirts of town, Jacob came upon a well, probably to be understood as the same community water source at which his mother Rebekah had impressed Abraham's servant years before (Genesis 24). Jacob's appearance at the

⚑ **More on context:** Genesis 29 is the opening act of a larger literary unit usually assigned to the Yahwist source, or to an edited composite of material from the Yahwist (J) and the Elohist (E). The unit, stretching from Genesis 29–31, is bound together by at least three running themes.

The first theme is an ongoing battle of wits between Jacob and Laban, his mother's brother. Jacob had slickly managed to manipulate his way through life until he got to Haran, but there he met his match in chicanery by having to deal with his deceptive and conniving uncle Laban. Although Jacob would ultimately gain the upper hand, he endured many trials along the way.

The second theme has to do with Jacob becoming the father of 11 sons and at least one daughter while in Haran, with their births coming through convoluted circumstances involving four different women. Again Jacob the manipulator found the sandal on the other foot as he became a pawn of his two wives.

The third theme is seen in an ongoing testimony that God was involved in all of the previous encounters, blessing Jacob in his dealings with Laban and "opening the womb" of Leah or Rachel at certain times.

well fits into the familiar betrothal-type scene, but with several twists befitting Jacob's unique personality.

First, Jacob alone moved the stone cover from the well, something ordinarily done by several men and only after all had gathered, ensuring that all shared equally in the use of the water. Jacob's action suggests that he was strikingly strong, which may come as a surprise since he has previously been described as a smooth-skinned homebody and possibly no physical match for his brother Esau. While Jacob's action appears chivalrous, it also shows that he had no qualms about violating custom in the service of his own interests (vv. 1-12).

Second, we recall that Abraham's servant had stood by while Rebekah drew water for his caravan of camels, but Jacob eagerly drew water for the flock of animals Rachel had brought to the well. Was Jacob simply being gallant and generous, or trying to impress the beautiful Rachel? Knowing Jacob, we are inclined to believe the latter.

After his long and lonely sojourn in the wilderness, Jacob was overcome with emotion to learn that the captivating Rachel was his cousin. Following her home, he received a warm and happy welcome from Rachel's father Laban, even though he arrived empty-handed, unlike Abraham's servant, who had brought rich gifts in the quest for a wife for Isaac (vv. 13-14).

Laban's initial warmth—"Surely you are my bone and my flesh!"—would prove a sharp contrast to the cold duplicity that would follow.

TWO WOMEN, ONE LOVE
(vv. 15-20)

Hospitality can only last for so long without some sort of official arrangement. So, after Jacob had stayed for a month with Laban's family—a time in which he apparently pitched in and did chores with the rest of them—Laban sought to engage the industrious young man in a binding contract. His query, "Why do you serve me for nothing?" was an opening bid in negotiating the wages he would have to pay for Jacob's continued labor.

Perhaps the narrator intentionally built irony into Laban's question about why Jacob would "serve" him for nothing. The reader knows by now that Jacob served no one, including God, for any purpose that did not serve himself—but he was willing to do what he had to do to get what he wanted.

What Jacob wanted was Rachel, Laban's daughter, but he knew that Laban would demand a steep price for her hand.

Fleeing Esau, Jacob had apparently left home with little in the way of money or other resources. His family's wealth was in livestock, which he could not conveniently transport while on the run. Later, as Jacob prepared to cross the Jordan back into Canaan, he would thank God that his family and wealth had grown even though "with only my staff I crossed this Jordan" on his way to Haran (32:10).

With no money to pay as a bride price, Jacob offered to indenture himself to Laban for seven years as payment for the woman he loved. In the course of negotiations, Jacob was well aware that Laban had an older daughter, so he carefully specified that his labor would be in exchange "for your younger daughter, Rachel" (v. 18). Laban agreed to the transaction: "It is better that I give her to you than that I should give her to any other man: stay with me" (v. 19).

We learned earlier that Rachel's older sister was named Leah, and that she was apparently less attractive than Rachel. The text mentions only her eyes, which are ambiguously described as "tender" (NET) or "delicate," though the NRSV has "lovely" (v. 18).

Whether Leah's eyes are to be thought of as glamorous or listless, she was clearly no match for Rachel, who is portrayed as both shapely in form and beautiful in appearance. The NRSV muddles the translation, describing her as "graceful and beautiful," though the text clearly comments on both her figure (literally, "beautiful of form/outline") and her overall comeliness ("beautiful of appearance").

While Rachel's physical appeal is the only characteristic given by the text, we have no way of knowing what other intangibles may have attracted Jacob to her. The narrator leaves no doubt, however, that Jacob was deeply smitten with Rachel. The seven years of labor seemed like a few days, we are told, "because of his love for her" (v. 20).

For Reflection: *Jacob's offer of seven years' labor for the privilege of marrying Rachel suggests something about the depth of his desire for her. How many of us would pay seven years' wages for the privilege of marrying our spouse?*

A HONEYMOON SURPRISE
(vv. 21-25)

⬇ A little ambiguity: Jacob's demand that Laban "Give me my bride that I may go in to her" (v. 21) translates a rather graphic Hebrew phrase commonly used to describe intercourse.

The same expression is found in Genesis 38, where Judah arranged to have sex with his widowed daughter-in-law Tamar, who was disguised as a prostitute. He propositioned, "Come, let me come in to you," and she replied "What will you give me that you may come in to me?" (38:16, NRSV). The NET translates more straightforwardly as "to have sex with you."

In the story of Jacob's marriage, his readiness for sex sets up the story of what happens on his wedding night.

Now for the twist: Jacob labored for seven years in order to win his bride, a long stretch in which he could do nothing more than make eyes at her. Jacob then insisted that Laban give him Rachel so they could begin married life. "Give me my wife, that I may go in to her" may sound crass, but Jacob was tired of waiting. He could appropriately identify Rachel as his "wife," for betrothals were binding.

The manner of Jacob's request seems rather crude. "Give me my wife," he said, "my time is up and I want to go in to her" (v. 21). The Hebrew expression translated "go in" (or "go into") was a common way of saying "have sex with her." ⬇

The crassness of Jacob's request may be the narrator's way of emphasizing Jacob's eagerness to consummate the marriage, perhaps without looking closely at his bride. After a day of wedding festivities in which men and women were largely separate, and after an evening banquet that may have involved some heavy drinking, Laban brought a veiled Leah into Jacob's dark tent instead of Rachel.

The narrator says nothing about Rachel's whereabouts or what she was thinking, only that Jacob slept that night with Leah, not realizing until morning's light that his bedmate was the older, unwanted sister.

> 🔯 **Really?** A rabbinic tradition later claimed that Rachel was in on the charade, hid beneath the marriage bed, and spoke or moaned at appropriate times so Jacob would hear her voice in the darkness—an unlikely story, given the severe jealousy that arose between the sisters.

The narrator has skillfully indicated that Jacob finally got his comeuppance. Although he was younger, he had tricked his way into receiving the birthright and blessing that rightfully belonged to the older brother. Now, though he had bargained for the younger sister, he was tricked into wedding the older one. Poetic justice was done. As Jacob deceived his blind father who depended on touch, he in turn had been flummoxed by darkness and an over-reliance on feel. Perhaps Leah had spoken as if she were Rachel, even as Jacob had claimed to be Esau. 🔯

ONE BRIDE, OR TWO?
(vv. 26-30)

When Jacob complained, Laban was unapologetic, insisting that local custom dictated that the older sister must marry first. Laban was not averse to having his hard-working son-in-law marry Rachel, too—something custom did allow—but it would cost Jacob an additional seven years of labor.

It is unlikely that Jacob had to wait an additional seven years before marrying Rachel: Laban asked only that he "finish this daughter's bridal week" (literally, "complete the period of seven for this one"), at which time he could marry Rachel, even though she came with an obligation to work for Laban an additional seven years. Jacob ended up getting two wives instead of one, but not two for the price of one. 🔯

> 🔯 **Parenthetical notes:** You will note the parenthetical indications that Laban gave each of his daughters possession of their respective handmaids: Zilpah to Leah and Bilhah to Rachel. This information will become important later, as both Rachel and Leah insist that Jacob have sex with their handmaids in an effort to sire children they can call their own—actions that recall childless Sarah's insistence that Abraham beget a child by her handmaid Hagar (Gen. 16:1-4).

Notice that neither woman is given a voice in the story. Today, we would judge that both women were mistreated by having the course of their lives determined for them, being "sold" to Jacob in return for his labor. For Leah it appears worse, because she is clearly less favored. The narrator emphatically tells us that Jacob loved Rachel. On the other hand, if Leah's "weak eyes" might have prevented her from finding a husband (she had gone more than seven years beyond marriageable age with no prospects), the arrangement might ultimately have served her well.

Still, we are left to wonder what the women thought about the arrangement. Was Rachel as in love with Jacob as he was with her? Was she aware of Laban's plans before the wedding? Did she cooperate willingly?

And how did Leah feel about this arrangement? Did she want to marry Jacob? Did she feel justified in participating in a marriage by deceit?

> **For Reflection:** *We don't know the answer to the above questions, but they can lead us to examine our own motives in our relationships with others. In our marriages and other relationships, do we seek others' good, or focus on our own needs? Do we relate to others with honesty, or harbor hidden agendas?*

The story of Jacob and Laban, Leah and Rachel is not a pretty one. It is hard for us to find redeeming qualities in the multiple layers of deceit and the ways in which people were manipulated like pawns. Yet, before all was said and done, something good emerged: Jacob and his wives would produce children who would become known as the fathers of the 12 tribes of Israel.

Despite our failures and foibles, our manipulations and machinations, God still manages to work through us: imagine the thought.

THE HARDEST QUESTION
What's the issue with Leah's eyes?

Translations of Gen. 29:17 differ in their description of Leah, who is said to have had distinctive eyes. But what made them so notable?

The Hebrew word used to describe Leah's eyes is *rakôt*, an adjective that means "tender," "soft," or "delicate." The word could possibly indicate that Leah's vision was poor, so that she squinted a lot, or that her eyes were particularly sensitive to light, but the narrator's intent is unclear.

Some translators take the term to be a derogatory description of her appearance, and her lack of marital prospects seems to underscore this view. Thus, the NIV and NAS95 translations say that Leah had "weak" eyes, and the HCSB (for no apparent reason) says they were "ordinary," with a footnote indicating the literal meaning is "tender," a relatively ambiguous reading followed by the KJV and NET. The NRSV stretches the translation in the other direction to say her eyes were "lovely."

Some commentators suggest that a reference to Leah's "tender eyes" might have been a backhanded compliment, implying that Leah's eyes were her only attractive feature—similar to someone promoting a blind date by saying she has a great personality. On the other hand, it seems most likely that her "tender eyes" were perceived as a detriment.

Whatever allure there may or may not have been in Leah's eyes, she apparently paled in comparison to Rachel, who is said to have had both a shapely figure and a pretty face.

Genesis 32:22-32

WRESTLING FOR A BLESSING

Then the man said,
"You shall no longer be called Jacob, but Israel,
for you have striven with God and with humans, and have prevailed."
—Genesis 32:28

Have you ever felt that you were wrestling with God over some issue, perhaps hoping for a particular outcome in business or romance, or struggling to understand why some tragedy has come into your life? We may plead, argue, or bargain with God, but few can claim to have engaged the divine in hand-to-hand combat.

Jacob could, and he lived to tell about it.

ONE FIGHT AFTER ANOTHER

Previous lessons have given us glimpses into the life of Jacob, the trickiest of the patriarchs. We have seen how Jacob finally met his match in Laban, an avaricious uncle who duped Jacob into marrying both of his daughters, though Jacob wanted only one.

We now fast-forward through a number of years during which Jacob and Laban continued their battle of wits. Jacob worked 14 years to pay the bride price for his two wives, then six more years for wages. With divine help via a dream, he bred the sheep and goats to produce either solid or striped/speckled/dark offspring, depending on which one Laban had allotted him as wages. In this manner Jacob acquired considerable holdings in livestock despite Laban's repeated insistence on changing their working agreement (30:25-43).

While increasing his flocks, Jacob also sired quite a brood of children, though he found himself in the uncomfortable position of being subject to the machinations of the women in his life. His primary wives, Rachel and Leah, conspired

> 🌀 **The big picture:** The story of Jacob's encounter with the "man of God" has similarities to both the Yahwist (J) and Elohist (E) sources, and scholars are divided about how to attribute it. The larger section in which the present text appears can be seen as the meat in a literary sandwich designed to emphasize the transforming effect of Jacob's very personal encounter with God at the Jabbock:
>
> *A fearful Jacob prepares to meet Esau (32:1-21).*
>
> *A determined Jacob meets and wrestles with God (32:22-32).*
>
> *A transformed Jacob meets Esau (33:1-17).*

to shuttle him back and forth between their beds and those of their handmaids (Bilhah and Zilpah), leaving him little to say about it. In the process, he fathered 11 sons and at least one daughter while in Haran (29:31–30:24). 🌀

As Jacob's household and the size of his flocks grew, his uncle Laban's attitude toward him soured. Bolstered by a word from God, Jacob decided to gather his wives, flocks, and other possessions in preparation for a return to his homeland (31:1-13). Knowing Laban would not want him to leave, Jacob led his considerable company out under cover of darkness, not knowing that his wife Rachel had stolen her father's household idols. When Laban discovered they were gone, he and a group of relatives pursued Jacob, catching up after a week's pursuit. After a heated exchange in which both men traded charges of stealing from the other, they reached an understanding, swore oaths to keep peace between them, and erected a mound of stones as a witness (31:14-55).

Finally free of their ties to Haran, Jacob and his large family continued their journey south along the eastern side of the Jordan River, moving as quickly as their sizeable flocks would allow them. At some point they stopped to camp near the fords of the Jabbok, a tributary of the Jordan about 20 miles north of the Dead Sea.

As they drew closer to Canaan, Jacob had turned his thoughts to another dangerous relative: his brother Esau. Would he still be angry after all these years? After a brief and mysterious encounter with angels, Jacob assumed he had stumbled upon God's camp, and named the place Mahanaim, meaning "two camps"—perhaps thinking of his camp and God's (32:1-2).

The visit apparently encouraged Jacob, and he sent messengers to his brother Esau (32:3-8), who had relocated to Edom, a rocky desert land south of the Dead Sea (a number of references identify Esau with Edom and as the ancestor of the Edomites [25:30; 36:1, 8, 19, 43]). Still afraid of Esau and showing surprising humility, Jacob referred to Esau as "my lord Esau" and to himself as "your servant Jacob."

⬦ **Praying for deliverance:** Jacob's prayer in 32:9-12 is very similar in form to some of the psalms of lament. The prayer is couched in humility, but still contains manipulative elements, as Jacob uses God's own words in hopes of gaining protection, addressing his prayer to the god "who said to me, 'Go back to your country and your relatives, and I will make you prosper'" (32:9b).

In his prayer, however, Jacob did finally acknowledge his heritage and his place in the divine scheme to make Abraham's descendants like the sand of the sea. This is in contrast to Gen. 28:20-22, where he had ignored those promises to focus on personal interests for provision and safekeeping.

The only aspect of God's promise to Jacob in Genesis 28 not yet fulfilled was a safe return to his homeland, for which Jacob prayed, reminding God of the divine promise that his descendants would be like the sand of the sea, a promise that Jacob presumed would require God to protect the mothers and children in his family.

When Jacob's envoys reported that Esau had set out to meet Jacob with a militia-sized retinue of 400 men, Jacob's initial response was to take defensive measures. He divided his family and property into two camps in hopes that one could escape if the other was attacked (another possible explanation of the place name "Mahanaim"). His second response was to pray for deliverance (32:9-12). Then, in an effort to placate his brother, Jacob sent a large gift of valuable livestock ahead of him (32:13-21), led by servants and spaced out in several groups for maximum effect. ⬦

> **For Reflection:** *Jacob's dysfunctional family life did not end when he moved away from his parents and their competing partialities. Indeed, with two primary wives, two secondary wives, and a dozen children prone to squabbling, it got even more complicated. Have you ever had to be the one to keep peace in your family? Was it worth the effort?*

WRESTLING FOR SURVIVAL
(vv. 22-25)

At this point Jacob did a surprising thing. During the night he moved his entire camp across the ford to the south side of the Jabbok (vv. 22-23). Then, apparently, he returned to the northern bank to remain alone through the night.

Why? Was Jacob being a coward, hanging back and leaving his family to face Esau without him? Did Jacob feel the need of some time in seclusion, perhaps to

> ♦ **Jacob's opponent:** It has often been suggested that the story of Jacob at
> the Jabbok has its roots in an old story about a river demon who would threaten
> travelers attempting to cross the ford, much like the trolls who guard the bridge
> in the fairy tale "Three Billy Goats Gruff." There is little literary evidence of such
> beliefs, however, and besides, Jacob had apparently crossed the ford multiple times
> without incident.

pray again for deliverance? We can't answer the question, nor can we fully explain what happened next.

A man appeared in the darkness, we are told, who "wrestled with him until daybreak" (v. 24). The Hebrew word for "wrestle" is a verbal form of the same root that means "dust." Literally, it means "to get dusty." That's what happens when one wrestles in the dirt. ♦

Jacob's opponent is called "the man" throughout, but because we are familiar with the story, we know that the "man" (*'ish*) is apparently God in human form, but apparently with some self-imposed limitations. God had "stood by" Jacob at Bethel as he prepared to leave Canaan, and now meets Jacob again as he prepares to re-enter the land. In their first encounter, God had spoken only words of blessing. This time, God attacked.

We are not told at what point Jacob recognized that he was wrestling with a divine adversary. Initially, he may have thought his assailant was Esau. The account of the wrestling is very brief, though we are led to believe that the opponents were evenly matched and the struggle lasted through the night.

That Jacob should prove to be a strong opponent is not surprising. We previously learned that he could move a heavy stone well cover by himself (Gen. 29:1-10), and his tenacity was persistent. As daybreak ("the rising of the dawn") drew near, Jacob's opponent saw that he "did not prevail" against Jacob through pure wrestling, so he struck a blow in the hollow of Jacob's thigh and dislocated his hip (v. 25).

The word translated as "strike" can also mean "touch," and some read this to mean that God exercised supernatural power by simply touching Jacob's hip and putting it out of joint. Since the opponent is clearly portrayed as being unable to prevail and thus self-limited in some way, however, perhaps we are to assume that he maneuvered Jacob into a vulnerable position, then struck his hip in such a way as to put it out of joint.

WRESTLING FOR A BLESSING
(32:26-32)

While the hip dislocation would have been extremely painful, Jacob maintained his hold and refused to let go, even though "the man" reminded him that dawn was breaking. It was widely believed that anyone who saw God's face would die, so God's request to be released was for Jacob's benefit. Jacob, however, seemed to have sensed his opponent's divine nature, and was so determined to receive a blessing from him that he was willing to risk his life in the effort (v. 26).

Jacob's resolve to receive a blessing is punctuated by two questions about names. God first asked Jacob's name, which he readily supplied, and God then gave him a new name: "You shall no longer be called Jacob, but Israel, for you have striven with God and with humans, and have prevailed" (v. 28).

"Israel" can mean "God fights," but it could also be taken to mean something akin to "he fought (with) God." Given the context, the latter seems more likely: it commemorates that Jacob had struggled with God as well as with men, and prevailed.

Unlike the stories of Jacob's grandfather, which consistently call him Abraham after his name was changed from Abram, later narratives refer to Jacob/Israel by both names.

Jacob was not satisfied to receive a new name of his own; he wanted to know the name of his adversary. Does this mean he was still uncertain with whom he was wrestling, or that he wanted God to reveal a more personal name that might grant Jacob some advantage? We cannot be sure, and his opponent deflected the question.

Jacob did not prevail enough to learn the name of his attacker, but he did win a blessing. God refused to reveal a name, but bestowed a blessing on Jacob, and that's all we know about how the match ended (v. 29).

Perhaps we are to presume that there had been enough light for Jacob to catch a shadowy glimpse of his opponent's face, for Jacob named the place "Peniel" (more commonly spelled "Penuel"), which means "face of God." Proud of having survived the encounter, Jacob said "I have seen God face to face, and my life has been preserved" (v. 30).

One of the most vivid images in all of scripture is the next one, told with bare-bones simplicity: "And the sun broke out on him as he crossed over Penuel, limping on his hip" (v. 31). Jacob may have seen God and survived, but he did not emerge unmarked. ⬧

⏻ **Been wrestling lately?** How long has it been since we have wrestled with God? Do our prayers come too easy to reflect any spiritual struggle? Is our faith something out on the periphery of our lives?

God engaged Jacob in battle precisely to gain his attention, to bless him with his presence, and to lock him into a purpose for living that was bigger than Jacob's own selfish goals. Wrestling with God is not always a pleasant experience, but it is through such encounters that God molds us and makes us to become people who are worthy of blessing and capable of passing on that blessing to others.

Olympians do not win gold medals without years of toil and struggle and pain. Christians do not experience the depth of God's blessing unless they are willing to wrestle with life's struggles and find energy in their wounds to feel the touch of God, to see God face to face. Wrestling with God will not win us gold medals and the accolades of the world, but it will keep us in touch with the one who made the world, and who calls us to be a blessing in the world.

> **For Reflection:** *Jacob was wounded in his wrestling with God, but in transformative ways. Sometimes our greatest blessings come through our deepest wounds. We should not argue that God causes all of our wounds, as he caused Jacob's, but when we are alone in the night, when we are wounded by life, we are more likely to focus on the most important priorities. When we are hurting or realize how badly we need help, we may be more inclined to seek the presence of the one who is our ultimate help. Has this proven true in your life?*

WRESTLING FOR A LESSON

Jacob's struggle with God has the potential for speaking to believers on several levels. We recall that Jacob's encounter with God was preceded by a prayer for deliverance (32:9-12), followed by the employment of a defensive strategy designed to protect his family. Jacob believed in praying for divine aid, but also in doing what he could for himself.

The nocturnal wrestling match with God, in some ways, combines both prayer and action. Jacob physically struggled with God, while also engaging in a conversation designed to elicit a blessing from God.

Few of us could claim to have grappled with God in a physical sense, but Jacob's encounter at the Jabbok reminds us that God comes to meet us on our own level, in our own imperfections, where we are—and that God's desire is to bless us.

Jacob's exchange with God on the subject of names reminds us that God knows our names. God knew Jacob's name without asking, but wanted the cunning patriarch to confess his nature as one who overreaches. The new name God gave honored Jacob's continued willingness to reach beyond what was expected. As Jacob had struggled with men, so he had struggled with God.

Finally, it could be worth considering the notion that God can break into our lives at any time and lead us in new directions. Jacob apparently had few thoughts beyond protecting himself and his family when he encountered the unexpected, mysterious presence of God. He was still walking when he emerged from the encounter, but his limp was a clear reminder that his life had been changed forever.

For Reflection: *Like Jacob's opponent, Christ came to earth as both God and man, living an intentionally self-limited human existence, and engaging worldly power for the benefit of humankind. Do you think God's appearance to Jacob in human form might help us imagine Jesus' role as both human and divine?*

THE HARDEST QUESTION
Why did Rachel steal her father's gods?

The story about Rachel stealing her father's household gods is curious on several fronts. On the one hand, we are not surprised that Laban worshiped other gods. Joshua 24:2 claimed that Abraham's father worshiped the moon god, known as Nanna back in Ur, and as Sîn in Haran: Nanna/Sîn was prominently worshiped in both cities. Abraham was called to leave Haran and follow Yahweh, but there is no story indicating that other family members changed their allegiance to the Mesopotamian gods.

When Jacob and Laban finally made some sort of peace, Jacob said "May the God of Abraham and the gods of Nahor judge between us" (31:53; a later scribe added "the God of their father" in an attempt to tone down the polytheistic overtones), indicating an awareness that Laban worshiped other gods.

It is not uncommon for archaeologists to uncover small clay figurines from private homes in the ancient Near East, including those once occupied by Israelites. Many of them feature female figures with large or multiple breasts, presumably to promote fertility. Such images are often identified as women's household gods, but the idols mentioned here are clearly denoted as belonging to Laban.

Why did Rachel want the images? Had she not converted to follow Yahweh, or was Jacob (as we might expect) not very outspoken about his beliefs? Did Rachel trust the power of the gods to help her, or think Laban would be impotent without them? If she had no personal faith in them, did she want to get in one final dig at the man who had forced her into a dual and conflicted marriage when she could have had Jacob for herself?

We don't know what Rachel's motivation was, but she took the gods and successfully hid the images from her angry father when Jacob gave permission for him to search the camp, swearing that anyone found to have stolen them would not live. Compounding her theft with a lie, Rachel hid the small idols beneath her saddle and sat on them, claiming she was on her period and couldn't get up (31:31-35).

Whether Jacob ever knew that Rachel had stolen the gods, we do not know, but his declaration that the thief would not live was fulfilled. Some time later, as they journeyed near Bethlehem, Rachel gave birth to another son, but died in the process (35:16-20). She wanted to name the child Ben-oni, meaning "son of my sorrow," but Jacob named him Benjamin, "son of the right hand."

Genesis 37:1-4, 12-28

SELLING JOSEPH

Now Israel loved Joseph more than any other of his children,
because he was the son of his old age;
and he had made him a long robe with sleeves.
—Genesis 37:3

If you have ever seen Andrew Lloyd Webber's musical *Joseph and the Amazing Technicolor Dreamcoat*, you've seen how Webber and lyricist Tim Rice wove the disparate stories of Jacob's son Joseph and his brothers into a cohesive story. The musical takes significant liberties with the account, as one might expect, but its playful mix of differing genres of music could remind the reader of the various strands of tradition that go into the Joseph narrative—and what a narrative it is.

While we normally think of Genesis 37–50 as the story of Joseph, the text is careful to tell us it is the story of *Jacob's* family: "This is the story of the family of Jacob" (37:2). And, while Joseph has the starring role, Joseph's brothers play a significant part in the story. Father Jacob looms in the background throughout the story until he resurfaces near the end, insists on adopting Joseph's offspring as his own (47:29–48:22), and blesses (or condemns) each of his sons while predicting the future of their families (49:1-28). After Jacob's death, his sons carry his body (according to his instructions) back to Canaan for burial in the family tomb at Macpelah (49:29–50:13), but they return to Egypt.

Though Jacob haunts the background, the lead character in our text for today is Joseph—and Joseph is in trouble.

A FAVORITE SON
(vv. 1-4)

The story begins with Jacob, having left Haran and surviving a surprisingly happy encounter with his brother Esau, settling into the land of Canaan, where he lived as a sojourner among the land's native peoples, probably near Hebron (v. 1, cf. 35:27).

We learn that Joseph is now 17 years old, so time enough had passed for the family to be at home in the land. Joseph, like his brothers, worked as a shepherd. He appears to have served a sort of apprentice role. Literally, "he was a lad with the sons of Bilhah and Zilpah, his father's wives." ⬧ His primary function may have been to serve as an errand boy, shuttling messages and possibly provisions back and forth between Jacob's home base and the brothers' temporary field quarters.

Whether Jacob's intent had been for Joseph to keep an eye on his brothers or whether he took it upon himself to report on their behavior is unclear. In either case, the text says that Joseph brought a "bad report" of them to his father (v. 2). Nothing more is said about it, but we may assume the older brothers would would not have been pleased.

Their irritation over Joseph's snitching, however, was nothing compared to all the brothers' resentment of Joseph because of their father's obvious favoritism. Jacob must have known the perils of partiality. His brother Esau had been his father's favorite, while he had been his mother's pride and joy (25:28). Nevertheless, Jacob carried the dysfunction into the next generation. Joseph was the first son born to his favorite wife, Rachel, after a wait of many years, and Jacob openly favored Joseph over his other children.

Jacob's preferential treatment of Joseph included the gift of a special cloak (v. 3). It was probably not "many-colored" (a tradition that began with the early Greek translation), but long-sleeved or possibly "embroidered." The same expression is used to describe the robe worn by Tamar, David's daughter, when she was raped by her brother Amnon (2 Samuel 13).

Whatever fashion statement the outfit might have made, the point is that Joseph's robe was notably more special than the ordinary garments worn by his brothers. Jacob's overt show of favoritism to Joseph did not play well with his siblings, "who hated him, and could not speak peaceably to him" (v. 4).

> **For Reflection:** *Have you seen (or felt) the results of parental favoritism in your family, or others? Have you ever seen anything good come out of it?*

A HATED BROTHER
(vv. 5-11)

The brothers' antipathy grew even deeper when Joseph began experiencing vivid dreams, and then reporting them to the rest of the family (v. 5). The first dream took place in a freshly harvested grain field, where Joseph's sheaf of grain suddenly stood up and the brothers' sheaves came and bowed down to it (vv. 6-7). Predictably incensed by the notion that Joseph would rule over them, the brothers "hated him even more because of his dreams and his words" (v. 8).

A second dream was even more grandiose. Joseph claimed to have seen the sun, moon, and 11 stars all bowing down to him (v. 9). The sun and moon clearly represent his parents, though Joseph's mother was dead, and the 11 stars his brothers. Understandably, the brothers' jealousy toward Joseph grew, and even his father Jacob offered a verbal rebuke, though he took no action, and "kept the matter in mind," no doubt wondering what the dream might mean (vv. 10-11).

> **For Reflection:** *The implication of the story is that Joseph's dreams stood out from ordinary dreams as divine hints about Joseph's future. We certainly can't assume that the nocturnal workings of our subconscious minds are all messages from God, but have you ever had dreams that either troubled you or gave you hope?*

A FUTURE SLAVE
(vv. 12-28)

With fraternal enmity fully established, the narrator fast-forwards to another day and perhaps another season, when Joseph's brothers were off pasturing the flocks near Shechem. Rains in Israel are seasonal, and shepherds could wander far from home in search of pastureland for their flocks. Jacob's brothers, according to the story, had indeed traveled far: from Jacob's camp near Hebron, Shechem would have been more than 50 miles to the north, a journey of at least two or three days by foot. The brothers could have kept the flocks there for weeks or perhaps months at a time, so Jacob would have cause to seek a periodic report on the welfare of his sons and of the sheep and goats. It's not surprising, then, that he dispatched Joseph to check on his brothers and bring back a report (vv. 12-14).

Joseph successfully made his way to Shechem, but could not find his brothers. When a local man found him wandering around the area and asked what he was up to, Joseph indicated that he was looking for his brothers. In typical storytelling style, it just happened that the man knew the brothers, and had overheard them discussing a plan to move the flocks toward Dothan, another 15 miles to the north and slightly west (vv. 15-17).

Another day's journey and Joseph saw his brothers in the distance. Unfortunately, they also saw him coming across the fields. Some of his brothers proposed that they kill the troublesome dreamer and throw him into a pit, telling their father that a wild animal had killed the boy. Then "we shall see what will become of his dreams," they said (vv. 18-19). Reuben, the oldest brother, reportedly demurred, suggesting only that they throw him into a pit without hurting him. He must have implied that they would leave him in the pit, though the narrator says Reuben secretly planned to rescue Joseph and take him home (vv. 20-22).

Reuben's plan prevailed, though some brothers still had blood on their minds. When Joseph arrived, they stripped off his special coat and threw him into a pit originally dug as a well or cistern but that was currently dry (vv. 23-24).

As the brothers left Joseph in the pit and sat down to celebrate the upstart's comeuppance with a meal, a caravan of Ishmaelite traders happened to pass by on their way from Gilead (east of the Sea of Galilee) to Egypt, loaded down with various goods. It's likely that two different traditions have been combined in the story, for now it is Judah who speaks up to save Joseph's life, rather than Reuben, suggesting that they sell him to the Ishmaelites. In doing so they would not only avoid bloodguilt, but also make some money in the process.

The brothers agreed—apparently while Reuben was absent—and when a group of Midianite traders came by, they pulled Joseph from the pit and sold him for 20 pieces of silver (vv. 25-28). The arrival of the Midianites further suggests that multiple versions of the story have been combined, but it's also possible that the narrator used "Ishmaelite" and "Midianite" interchangeably as a reference to nomadic traders. ♿

In the meantime, Reuben returned to find Joseph gone and his plans for rescue thwarted. To cover their crime, the brothers slaughtered a goat and dipped Joseph's tunic in it, later showing it to Jacob as evidence that a wild beast had devoured his favorite son. Jacob became distraught, as one might expect, and would not be comforted (vv. 29-35).

⬧ **Who bought and sold Joseph?** If the narrative of vv. 25-28 sounds confusing, there's good reason for it. Who bought and sold Joseph: the Ishmaelites or Midianites?

The Ishmaelites' ancestry was traced to Abraham's first son, Ishmael, and the Midianites to a son of Abraham's second wife, Keturah. But both groups became known as largely nomadic people who made their living as traders. Through the years, the distinction seems to have diminished, and the terms sometimes appear interchangeable as a catch-all label for wandering merchants. Genesis is not the only place that happens: Judg. 24:8 identifies the raiders who Gideon defeated as both Midianites and Ishmaelites.

It's likely that two traditions may have been combined here. It has been suggested that Reuben's defense and the Midianite traders derived from the Elohist source (37:18, 21-22, 24-25a, 28a, 29-30), and Judah's intervention and Ishmaelite merchants came from an older story by the Yahwist (37:19-20, 23, 25b-27, 28b, 31-32).

Aside from the different names, we note that the Ishmaelites and Midianites seem to make separate appearances in the story. Even so, the discrepancies apparently didn't trouble the editor/narrator. He says the brothers sold Joseph to "the Ishmaelites," who carried him down to Egypt, where "the Midianites" sold him to a man named Potiphar, in Egypt (v. 36).

In either case, there is an unexpected connection. Joseph, the chosen son of Jacob, the chosen son of Isaac, the chosen son of Abraham, becomes captive to the unchosen descendants of his great-grandfather.

For Reflection: *Have you ever experienced such a shocking or tragic loss that no one could comfort you?*

A MODERN LESSON

The brothers' betrayal and merchandising of Joseph is a familiar and entertaining story, but what might modern believers gain from it?

We should first look to the narrator's purpose in telling the story. He wants us to see how God can take a bad thing (the selling of Joseph) and turn it into something good (the future deliverance of Jacob's family from famine). That does not make hurtful actions commendable, but illustrates a belief that God can orchestrate human events for divine purposes. Later, when Joseph had ascended to power in Egypt and Jacob had died, his brothers feared that Joseph might take

🔸 **God in the background:** Scholars often note that, though God is often mentioned in Genesis 37–50, the deity plays a less active role than in earlier patriarchal stories. While the narratives insist that God spoke directly to Abraham, Isaac, and Jacob, God never appeared directly to Joseph. The reader may assume that God sent messages to Joseph via dreams, and the narrator leaves no doubt that God was with Joseph and blessed him, but God's overt involvement shifts to the background.

For his part, Joseph built no altars to Yahweh as his forbears did, yet managed to serve Yahweh within a land of other gods. He did not hear the Abrahamic promise of progeny from God, but from Jacob, and then not until 48:3-4, 21-22. Thus, Terrence Fretheim has argued, "The human community now becomes responsible for the transmission of the word of God."[1]

The narrator's belief that providence was at work in Joseph's coming to Egypt is also apparent in 45:7-8, where Joseph told his brothers: "God sent me before you to preserve for you a remnant on earth, and to keep alive for you many survivors. So it was not you who sent me here, but God; he has made me a father to Pharaoh, and lord of all his house and ruler over all the land of Egypt."

vengeance on them, but he offered them forgiveness: "Even though you intended to do harm to me, God intended it for good, in order to preserve a numerous people, as he is doing today" (50:20). 🔸

If we live long enough, bad things will happen to us. Friends or family may treat us shabbily; colleagues in the workplace may undermine our advancement. We cannot always attribute poor treatment to God, as Joseph did, but we can believe that God can work in and through our open hearts to teach us, strengthen us, and ultimately bring something good from the situation.

> **For Reflection:** *Have you ever experienced an injury or personal trial that caused great pain, and yet you can say that you learned something—or even gained something positive—from the experience?*

Though it was not the author's primary intent, the story also reminds us of the dangers of family favoritism. When parents play favorites with their children—at any age—they sow seeds of jealousy, discord, and emotional issues that may play out over many years and repeat themselves in generations to come. Jacob apparently learned nothing from the pain of knowing that his father loved Esau more than him, and he passed that hurt on to his children by openly favoring Joseph over his brothers. Can we learn to do better?

THE HARDEST QUESTION
How does the Joseph novella fit into the larger Book of Genesis?

Genesis consists of two primary divisions, often called the "Primeval History" (chs. 1-11) and the "Patriarchal History" (chs. 12–50). Abraham is first introduced in a genealogy (11:27-32), but his story begins in earnest with ch. 12. Abraham's story continues until his death (25:7-11), interlaced with stories about Isaac.

Isaac takes center stage only briefly (25:19–28:9), and then mostly as a background character, for the narrator's primary interest is that he is Abraham's son and Jacob's father. Jacob's story comes to the fore at 28:10, continuing through ch. 35, though he doesn't die until the final chapter.

Family genealogies in Genesis often serve as framing devices to end one story and begin another, often relating in meaningful ways with both. In this case, the genealogy of Esau in ch. 36 is an appropriate introduction to chs. 37–50, because both Esau's genealogy and the following "generations of Jacob" narrative emphasize the transition from an individual to a people.

According to ch. 36, Esau became the progenitor of the Edomites, a people living south of the Dead Sea and frequently at odds with Israel (twice the genealogy says "Esau, he is Edom"). Now Jacob, enabled by the timely and God-enhanced efforts of his son Joseph, also grows to become a people. After Jacob's wrestling match with God at the Jabbok, God had given him the alternate name "Israel" (32:28). Through his children, father Israel becomes the Israelites. By the time we reach the end of the section, Jacob's 12 sons have multiplied to at least the fourth generation, which could have comprised a considerable multitude of people.

In this way, the Joseph story provides an appropriate end to the book of Genesis, which is primarily concerned with God's promise of progeny. But it also serves as an effective lead-in to the Book of Exodus, where the people of Israel have multiplied in Egypt, and the focus shifts to their consolidation as a nation and their quest to possess the Promised Land.

The final section of Genesis has long been recognized as a structured unit that includes material from disparate sources, but holds together well enough to be given titles such as "short story" or "novella." While the earlier narratives are often separate episodes bracketed by genealogies and stitched together by travel notes, chs. 37–50 appear to be a larger, more unified work.

It might be helpful to consider a rough outline of the "novella" as follows:

37:1-36
Joseph the dreamer predicts prominence but falls from favor with his brothers, who sold him as a slave bound for Egypt.

38:1-30
As Joseph toils in Egypt, life goes on in Canaan, where older brother Judah falls for a ploy by his daughter-in-law Tamar, who secures his heritage for him.

39:1–41:57
Joseph rides a roller coaster to power in Egypt.
- Joseph rises to the top in Potiphar's house, then to prison (39:1-23)
- Joseph rises to the top in prison, then to Pharaoh's palace (40:1-23)
- Joseph rises from dream interpreter to ruler in Pharaoh's palace (41:1-57).

42:1–45:28
A reunion with his brothers fulfills Joseph's dreams.
- Joseph's brothers beg to buy food but don't recognize Joseph, who speaks harshly but weeps privately, and tests his brothers' loyalty (42:1-38).
- Joseph's brothers beg again, and are frightened when Joseph brings them to his house for lunch, seating them according to age (43:1-43).
- Joseph tests the brothers' fraternal fidelity toward Benjamin, and they pass the test (44:1-34).
- Joseph tearfully reunites with his brothers and invites the whole clan to live in his care (45:1-28).

46:1–47:26
Israel comes to Egypt.
- Jacob sacrifices, receives a vision, and journeys with his family to Egypt (46:1-27).
- Joseph settles Jacob's family in the land of Goshen (46:28–47:12).
- Joseph uses stored grain to buy all of Egypt for Pharaoh (47:13-26).

47:27–50:26
An incipient nation emerges.
- Jacob adopts Joseph's sons (told in two versions) (47:27–48:22).
- Jacob's last words, of blessing and curse, look to the future (49:1-33).
- Jacob dies in Egypt but is buried in Canaan (50:1-14).
- Jacob's sons are truly reconciled (50:15-21).
- Joseph dies in Egypt, but his burial in Canaan is delayed (50:22-26).

We won't be able to consider all of these stories in this book, but will take a good look at two more significant passages, with some brief discussion of the narrative that holds them together.

NOTE

[1]Terrence Fretheim, "Genesis," in *The New Interpreter's Bible*, vol. 1 (Abingdon, 1994), 594.

Genesis 45:1-15

MAKING PEACE

And he kissed all his brothers and wept upon them;
and after that his brothers talked with him.
—Genesis 45:15

Have you ever "kissed and made up" with someone? A disruption in personal relationships can be exceedingly painful, especially when the other party is a spouse, a parent, a brother, or sister. Relational breakdowns can grow from innocent misunderstandings, from callous selfishness, from unhealthy competition, or other causes. Repairing relationships has to begin with a mutual desire for reconciliation and honest communication that openly confronts the issues and works toward resolution. That usually includes an apology—sometimes from both parties—and a promise to be more considerate going forward.

Making up can be hard to do, but it can also be awesome. Feeling the walls of resentment come down, receiving forgiveness, and embracing again can bring a renewed sense of closeness in a cleansing, life-giving experience.

For Reflection: *Break-up and make-up songs have been a mainstay of popular music through the years. How many can you remember?*

Many things can be forgiven, but do you think you could forgive someone who had stolen your favorite coat, kidnapped you, and sold you to a gang of slave-traders? If things had not turned out so well for Joseph, you have to wonder if the story would have ended differently.

A STORY OF SUCCESS

Fortunately, things did go surprisingly well, and a brief review is in order. After Joseph's brothers sold him to a caravan of traders, he was taken to Egypt and re-sold to a government official named Potiphar. As an honest and impressive young man, he advanced quickly and was given charge of Potiphar's estate before a false accusation from his master's wife landed him in prison (39:1-20).

Behind bars, Joseph's positive attitude and actions paid off again, as the head jailer soon put him in charge of the other prisoners. During his prison days, dreams returned to the story, along with Joseph's knack for interpreting them. The royal cupbearer promised to intercede for Joseph after he correctly explained a portentous dream, but failed to follow through (39:21–40:23). Fortunately, when the pharaoh had two troublesome dreams that none of his officials could interpret, the cupbearer remembered Joseph, who saw them as obvious indications that Egypt would enjoy seven years of plenty, followed by a famine of the same length. Joseph suggested a planned system of taxation to store surplus grain against the coming famine. The king, suitably impressed, set Joseph over the effort, a position second in power to the pharaoh alone (41:1-45). Joseph had gone from the pits to the Ritz.

Residents of nearby Canaan had no similar plan for food security, but they faced the same drought. In the second year of the famine, hunger brought Joseph's 10 older brothers to Egypt in search of food for Jacob's clan (42:1-5). They had no idea that their pesky younger sibling had risen to power there, and would not have recognized him as a fully-grown man, dressed in Egyptian style, bearing the Egyptian name Zaphenath-Paneah, and no doubt speaking in Egyptian.

Joseph, on the other hand, had no trouble identifying his older brothers in their common shepherd's garb. He seems to have struggled with his emotions, and forgiveness did not come quickly. Joseph was clearly touched, but did not yet trust the siblings who had sold him down the river Nile. Guessing that Benjamin would have become Jacob's new favorite, he tested the brothers to see if they showed more loyalty to his younger brother than they had to him.

Joseph first charged the brothers with espionage and held Simeon in jail while sending the other brothers home with sacks of grain that also contained the money they had paid. He pledged not to receive them again until the other nine returned with Benjamin (42:6-38). The family had to reach great extremity, and Judah had to plead with his father before he allowed Benjamin to go with them. After that visit, Joseph again wept secretly, but had his personal silver cup planted in Benjamin's bag of grain so he could accuse the brothers of theft (43:1–44:13). When Judah pleaded for his younger brother and offered to take any punishment upon himself, Joseph was convinced that the brothers deserved another chance (44:14-34).

> **For Reflection:** *Joseph's actions in exercising power over his brothers may seem vindictive. Do you think he was intentionally frightening them as a bit of revenge, or just testing their honesty and integrity?*

🔯 **A new name:** The ruling pharaoh gave to Joseph an Egyptian name when he was appointed to supervise the collection and storage of grain during the years of plenty, as well as the allocation of grain after the famine arrived (41:45). The name is rendered in Genesis as *Zaphenath-Paneah*, a Hebraized form of an Egyptian phrase of uncertain meaning. Some options may include "the god has said 'he will live,'" "the god speaks and lives," and "the man he knows." The precise meaning is less important than the official status as an Egyptian symbolized by the name.

At the same time, the pharaoh gave to Joseph an Egyptian wife, whose name was Asenath. As the daughter of a priest, she would have been of high status. A modern version of the name, "Osnat," is popular among Jews in Israel today.

Joseph and Asenath had two sons, Ephraim and Manasseh. While they may have also had Egyptian names, the names recorded in scripture are Hebrew. "Manasseh," the firstborn, was called "*menashsheh*," a participle form of the verb meaning "to forget," thus "he who brings about forgetfulness." Joseph reportedly said, "God has made me forget all my hardship and all my father's house" (41:51). Perhaps the son's name was designed to suggest that Joseph had forgotten his former troubles and come to terms with his life.

"Ephraim" is from a verb meaning "to bear fruit," and suggests fruitfulness or fertility. Joseph said, "For God has made me fruitful in the land of my misfortunes" (41:52). Much of the northern part of Israel later came to be known as Ephraim.

AN EMOTIONAL REUNION
(vv. 1-3)

At last, as in some modern reality TV shows, it was time for "the big reveal." Joseph invited his brothers to a private banquet with him. With his siblings bowing before him (as they had in his dream of the sheaves, 37:6-7), Joseph's emotions erupted: "Then Joseph could no longer control himself before all those who stood by him" (v. 1). Dismissing his Egyptian assistants, Joseph began to weep so loudly that he could be heard throughout the palace (v. 2). Joseph's tears must have been cathartic for him as he released long-held resentment toward his brothers, but it must have been equally confusing to them as the overbearing Egyptian official's stern visage dissolved into unfettered weeping.

"I am Joseph," he said, presumably in Hebrew. *"Is my father still alive?"* Can you imagine the shock? The brothers had answered that question on two previous occasions, but in a formal hearing and probably through an interpreter, when asked about *their* father. Now Joseph wanted to hear it again while also affirming kinship: "Is *my* father still alive?"

Joseph's brothers were dumbfounded, just as we might have been—so shocked that they ". . . could not answer him, so dismayed were they at his presence" (v. 3).

No wonder they were dismayed. They knew they were guilty, and Joseph was wailing loudly. How were they to know if it was love or anger that prompted his cries?

For Reflection: *How would you have reacted in Joseph's situation? What would you have felt, done, or said?*

A THEOLOGICAL ASSERTION
(vv. 4-8)

Joseph quickly moved to calm the brothers' fears, calling them closer so they could see him better and not be fooled by his Egyptian-style clothing, hair, and cosmetic enhancements. "I am your brother Joseph," he said, "the one you sold into Egypt" (v. 4). They knew it had to be true, because no one else would have known what they had done.

Apparently believing the brothers had suffered enough, Joseph assuaged their guilt and told them of his belief that God had turned their jealous treachery into something good. He would not have been positioned to save the family—and others—if he had not come to Egypt (vv. 5-8).

The brothers drew near, but the narrator grants them not another word until the end of the encounter, when they embraced, wept, and "his brothers talked with him." We don't know what they had to say, because the narrator is more interested in promoting his belief in God's prevailing providence. "God sent me before you . . ." (vv. 5, 7), he has Joseph say, "So it was not you who sent me here, but God . . ." (v. 8).

Should we imagine that Joseph fully believed it was all God's doing? There are Christians who call on texts like this one to insist that God determines everything that happens, both good and bad. "Everything happens for a reason" is a common expression that warrants closer examination. Should we blame God for others' behavior, for illness, accidents, or natural disasters, assuming that God orchestrates bad things to teach us good lessons? The narrator believed that God had brought good from the wrong Joseph's brothers had done, but that does not support a belief that God determines everything.

God is the source of goodness, not evil. Paul affirmed in Rom. 8:28 that: ". . . in all things God works for the good of those who love him," but we can credit God with working in our lives to transform pain into laughter or grief into grace without blaming God for the initial hurt.

For Reflection: *Have you heard others say, or said yourself, "Everything happens for a reason"? Do you believe that is true?*

A GRACE-FILLED MOMENT
(vv. 9-15)

The story concludes with forgiveness. It was long in coming, but Joseph eventually forgave his brothers. Once they got over the shock, they were willing to accept his forgiveness, though they remained insecure about their standing (witness their fear some years later following Jacob's death, 50:15-21). Joseph instructed them to return to Hebron and bring their father Jacob along with the entire clan to Egypt, promising to provide for them, their children, and their flocks throughout the remaining five years of famine (vv. 9-13). ♟

Words soon gave way to tears and hugs. Joseph embraced first his full brother Benjamin, then hugged and kissed (and no doubt slapped the back of) his other brothers, who finally emerged from their shocked silence and were able to talk with Joseph (vv. 14-15). What they said is not recorded, but we can be sure that the older brothers did all they could to express sorrow for their actions and gratitude for Joseph's forgiveness. Afterward, we like to think, they may have sat together and talked freely of wives and children, of various experiences through the years. Joseph, at least, had quite a few stories to tell!

Forgiveness doesn't work unless it is both freely given and freely received—without conditions. Only then can relationships be restored. Only then

♟ **A major switch:** Joseph not only forgave his brothers' wrong-doing, but also overwhelmed them with generosity. He told them to go home, pack their belongings, and return with his father, their families, and their flocks.

With the pharaoh's permission, he even sent wagons with them to make the move easier, as does an employer who takes care of a new employee's move. In addition, Joseph gave a set of new clothes to each of the brothers, though carrying on the tradition of partiality: Benjamin received five changes of clothes and 300 pieces of silver, 15 times the amount the other brothers had received in payment for Joseph.

Once the family arrived in Egypt, Joseph assigned them land in a part of the northwest Nile delta called "Goshen," a land so rich and fertile that it gave rise to the happy expression "land o' Goshen!" (vv. 16-24).

can love blossom. Only then can once-restrained persons relax and rejoice in the warmth of each other's presence.

> **For Reflection:** *While we cannot know for sure what was in Joseph's heart, one could argue that Joseph intentionally waited to show forgiveness until he thought his brothers were ready to receive it. Based on your experience, what settings or attitudes are needed before we can experience forgiveness?*

What do you think?

The story of Joseph and his brothers emphasizes forgiveness between persons. Can it also teach us something about the forgiveness that God offers? What is required if we are to know God's forgiveness?

Doesn't this text offer a continued challenge and promise to any of us who suffer from broken relationships? Jesus taught us that believers have a responsibility to take the initiative in seeking reconciliation (Matt. 5:24). Others may or may not respond to our efforts, but when we offer forgiveness—or an apology, if needed—the door to reconciliation is open, and the path beyond is one of hope.

> **For Reflection:** *Think back to a situation in which someone hurt you, and you found it hard to forgive. What obstacles keep us from offering forgiveness more freely? Are we afraid of something—perhaps rejection or vulnerability—or just too angry to let it go? Can you think of someone you need to forgive or someone from whom you need to seek forgiveness?*

THE HARDEST QUESTION
Was Joseph responsible for Israel's enslavement?

While we typically think of Joseph as Israel's savior, we also recognize that he was responsible for getting them to Egypt, where the Book of Exodus says they ultimately became slaves. But were they virtual slaves even before then, enslaved by Joseph himself?

The story says that after Joseph was appointed as Egypt's minister of agriculture, he used his authority to commandeer much of the grain harvest from seven years of plenty. Indeed, the text says he took *all* the grain, though it must be a reference to all the grain not needed for immediate consumption or replanting, or the people would have starved: "He gathered up all the food of the seven years when there was plenty in the land of Egypt, and stored up food in the cities; he stored up in every city the food from the fields around it. So Joseph stored up grain in such abundance—like the sand of the sea—that he stopped measuring it; it was beyond measure" (41:48-49).

When the famine arrived, Joseph was prepared to feed the world (41:53-57), but did not redistribute the grain freely, even to the Egyptian farmers who had raised it. He charged both the Egyptians and the people of nearby Canaan for rations of grain. In time, the text says, he had collected all the money and livestock in both Egypt and Canaan, leaving the people so in debt that they became virtual slaves in their own land. Consider this account, from the NET:

> But there was no food in all the land because the famine was very severe; the land of Egypt and the land of Canaan wasted away because of the famine. Joseph collected all the money that could be found in the land of Egypt and in the land of Canaan as payment for the grain they were buying. Then Joseph brought the money into Pharaoh's palace. When the money from the lands of Egypt and Canaan was used up, all the Egyptians came to Joseph and said, "Give us food! Why should we die before your very eyes because our money has run out?"
>
> Then Joseph said, "If your money is gone, bring your livestock, and I will give you food in exchange for your livestock." So they brought their livestock to Joseph, and Joseph gave them food in exchange for their horses, the livestock of their flocks and herds, and their donkeys. He got them through that year by giving them food in exchange for livestock.
>
> When that year was over, they came to him the next year and said to him, "We cannot hide from our lord that the money is used up and the livestock and the animals belong to our lord. Nothing remains before our lord except our bodies and our land. Why should we die before your very eyes, both we and our land? Buy us and our land in exchange for food, and we, with our land, will become Pharaoh's slaves. Give us seed that we may live and not die. Then the land will not become desolate."
>
> So Joseph bought all the land of Egypt for Pharaoh. Each of the Egyptians sold his field, for the famine was severe. So the land became Pharaoh's. Joseph made all the people slaves from one end of Egypt's border to the other end of it. But he did not purchase the land of the priests because the priests had an allotment from Pharaoh and they ate from their allotment that Pharaoh gave them. That is why they did not sell their land.
>
> Joseph said to the people, "Since I have bought you and your land today for Pharaoh, here is seed for you. Cultivate the land. When you gather in the crop, give one-fifth of it to Pharaoh, and the rest will be yours for seed for the fields and for you to eat, including those in your households and your little children." They replied, "You have saved our lives! You are showing us favor, and we will be Pharaoh's slaves."

So Joseph made it a statute, which is in effect to this day throughout the land of Egypt: One-fifth belongs to Pharaoh. Only the land of the priests did not become Pharaoh's. (47:13-26, NET)

Note that this occurred after Joseph had brought his family to Egypt. "so that you and your household, and all that you have, will not come to poverty" (45:11). The account in ch. 47 does not specify that Joseph's family was an exception to having to buy grain, noting that only the priests were exempt, receiving a fixed allowance from Pharaoh. We would assume that they were not impoverished, however, for the enslavement of the Egyptians is followed immediately by this observation: "Thus Israel settled in the land of Egypt, in the region of Goshen; and they gained possessions in it, and were fruitful and multiplied exceedingly" (47:27). Would they have been allowed to keep their property while native Egyptians were losing theirs?

A total of about 70 males from Jacob's family entered Egypt, according to 46:26-27, and the infertility that had plagued the first three generations became a thing of the past. By the time we reach the Book of Exodus, there were so many Hebrews that the new pharaoh felt compelled to control their population, for "the Israelites were fruitful and prolific; they multiplied and grew exceedingly strong, so that the land was filled with them" (Exod. 1:7).

If that is the case, why had they remained in Egypt? Having grown strong, and with the famine ended, why had they not returned to Canaan? Had they become enslaved to their newfound prosperity in Egypt, or did the ruling pharaohs not allow them to leave? Were they prosperous, but restricted in their movements?

In either case, the Israelites' prosperity in the heart of Egypt's fertile delta would have sown seeds of jealousy and enmity with their Egyptian neighbors, who had become impoverished and virtual slaves to the king while foreigners prospered on the best of their land.

Joseph had begun his career as a slave to an Egyptian, and ended his career by enslaving the Egyptians. It's no wonder that, when the opportunity arose, the Egyptians were more than happy to force the burgeoning population of Israelites into servitude.

Genesis 49:1-28

LAST WORDS

Judah, your brothers shall praise you;
your hand shall be on the neck of your enemies;
your father's sons shall bow down before you.
—Genesis 49:8

L ast words are important. Perhaps you have been present when a dying person uttered what turned out to be his last actual words, or perhaps you have brooded over the last thing someone important said to you before her death. For good or ill, a dying person's last words can affect the lives of those who remain.

Genesis 49 contains what were reportedly the last words of Jacob as he gathered his 12 sons around him to offer a last blessing—or critique. It's likely that these words owe more to a later writer's knowledge of the tribes than to an accurate historical record of a patriarch's actual words. Even so, the narrator's intent in constructing the passage has more to say than we might see on the surface. It explains why the tribe of Judah came to dominate the south, and why the tribes of Joseph's sons (Ephraim and Manasseh) came to dominate the north.

A quick look at this text also gives us an opportunity to reflect back on some parts of the patriarchal stories not included in the earlier lessons.

OCCASIONAL ANARCHS ...

We have noted in previous lessons that the Genesis stories include not only patriarchs and matriarchs to foster the blessing and further the promise of Abraham's descendants becoming "a great nation," but there were also "anarchs" whose actions threatened it.

Indeed, the biggest threat came from Yahweh, who was regarded as fully responsible for "opening" or "closing" a woman's womb. Yahweh promised Abraham descendants like the stars in the sky or the sand on the seashore, but did not grant Sarah a child until she was 90 years old (chs. 18, 21). After that, God further threatened the promise by commanding Abraham to sacrifice the long-awaited son (ch. 22).

Later, Isaac's wife Rebekah was childless for 20 years, and Jacob's wives Rachel and Leah struggled with barrenness until Yahweh saw fit to "open their wombs" and give them children.

While we may see this as reflecting negatively on God, the narrator saw it as a series of divine tests of the chosen men and women's faithfulness to Yahweh, and as a repeated proof of God's power. Though the promise was often threatened by obstacles, Yahweh proved true and always overcame the obstacles to fulfill the promise.

Abraham, the founding patriarch, also behaved in ways that threatened the promise. Twice, when traveling in another ruler's territory, he pretended that Sarah was his sister for fear that the king would kill him in order to take his wife. Both the pharaoh of Egypt (12:11-20) and King Abimelech of Gerar (20:1-18) desired Sarah—reportedly beautiful despite her senior citizen status—and took her into their harems for a period of time before Yahweh sent plagues upon them, leading to Sarah's restoration. Later, Abraham willingly participated in Yahweh's "test" of his faithfulness, binding Isaac to an altar and preparing to kill him before God provided a ram as an alternate sacrifice.

Isaac took after his father, according to 26:6-11, which reports that Isaac also valued his life over his wife's chastity. While residing in Gerar during a time of famine, he claimed that his wife Rebekah was his sister. As a result, King Abimelech—same name and country as in 20:1-18, but this time identified as a Philistine—was planning to take her into his harem. Before doing so, however, he saw Isaac fondling Rebekah in a non-sisterly way, and he realized what an offense he would have committed if he had taken her. In all three of these stories, the foreign kings seem much more concerned about committing a moral offense than the patriarchs who seemed willing to give up their wives to save their skin.

We could argue that both Jacob and Esau acted like anarchs in that Jacob stole Esau's blessing and made Esau so livid that he put his own life in jeopardy. But, one could also argue that Jacob was justified in taking the blessing away from Esau, who was clearly unfit to be the progenitor of Israel, and thus Jacob was preserving the blessing rather than working against it. It's unlikely, however, that such thoughts would have crossed Jacob's mind, for he looked out for himself.

While it's possible to put a positive spin on some of Jacob's endangering actions, the same cannot be said of Jacob's sons, several of whom put the family in serious jeopardy. This brings us to the last words of Jacob, who had something to say about his sons' behavior.

> **For Reflection:** *We don't often think of patriarchal personalities as anarchs, especially God. Why do you think the narrator portrayed Yahweh as one who could promise children to the patriarchal families, then test their patience by delaying their ability to conceive?*

BLESSINGS LOST
(vv. 1-7)

Reuben was the oldest of Jacob's sons (the first four sons were all born to Leah). He appears occasionally in the narratives. A story about him finding mandrakes and bringing them to his mother is a reminder that he was nearly grown before some of his younger brothers were born (30:14-17). On the positive side, one story claims that he intervened to save Joseph from being killed by his brothers (37:18-24), but there was a black mark that couldn't be erased. On one occasion, as Jacob led his large family on the long journey from Haran to Beersheba, and not long after Rachel had died, "Reuben went and lay with Bilhah his father's concubine, and Israel heard of it" (35:22).

Bilhah had been Rachel's handmaid. When Rachel appeared infertile, she insisted (twice) that Jacob impregnate Bilhah as a surrogate mother so she could claim the children. Bilhah then gave birth to Dan and Naphtali. Considering that Jacob had had two lead wives who had been extremely jealous sisters before Rachel's death, along with two secondary wives who had their own agendas, the family was dysfunctional enough already. Can you imagine the strife Reuben's actions could have caused?

Though nothing is said of Jacob's reaction in 35:22, he apparently never forgot it. When he gathered his sons for the final time, Reuben—as the oldest—was in line to receive the blessing of the firstborn and become the new leader of the family. We learn, however, that he had squandered that privilege. Jacob said to him:

> Reuben, you are my firstborn, my might and the first fruits of my vigor, excelling in rank and excelling in power. Unstable as water, you shall no longer excel because you went up onto your father's bed; then you defiled it—you went up onto my couch! (49:3-4)

Jacob's words indicate that Reuben had the talent needed to lead, but had squandered his position by sleeping with one of his father's wives, bringing shame upon all three of them. As it turned out, Reuben's descendants, whose allotment was on the east side of the Jordan, was one of the first tribes to disappear.

The next two sons in line for the blessing and the leadership role were Simeon and Levi. Perhaps they were trying to act in a leadership role when they put the entire family in danger of extermination through their treacherous actions at Shechem (ch. 34), but Jacob didn't see it that way.

That ugly story is rarely told, and it takes us back a bit, back to Jacob's first entry into Canaan. After making peace of a sort with Esau, Jacob stayed on the east side of the Jordan for a while before crossing the Jordan and setting up camp outside the city of Shechem (33:18). ♂

> ♂ Shechem: The city of Shechem was located on the northern edge of the central hill country in Israel, about 16 miles west of the Jordan. Shechem's inhabitants were called Hivites, one of the many ethnic groups that we generically refer to as Canaanites.

There Jacob bought a plot of land for the clan's camp, paying "100 pieces of money" to Hamor, the king of Shechem, a small city that claimed surrounding lands. He then built an altar and named it *El Elohe Israel*—"God, the God of Israel"—and all seemed to be well, until Dinah went out one day to visit with the women of the area. According to the text, which uses a rapid series of verbs, the king's son (also named Shechem) "saw" Dinah, then "he took her, and lay with her, and humbled her" (a literal translation).

The first two verbs can be used of ordinary marriage and sex, but the third one is from a root that means "to humble" or "to afflict," and it can be translated in the sense of sexual assault.

The story tells us nothing about Dinah's actions or her feelings, but the narrator clearly understood Shechem's action to be rape, and her brothers believed it to be the case.

Even so, the customs of the day may have led the king's son to feel entitled to take her into his house, just as the king of Egypt and the king of Gerar had felt entitled to take Sarah or Rebekah into their harems. Shechem was no typical rapist; he became smitten with Dinah, took her into his home, "And his soul was drawn to Dinah daughter of Jacob; he loved the girl, and spoke tenderly to her. So Shechem spoke to his father Hamor, saying, 'Get me this girl to be my wife'" (34:3-4, cf. 17, 26). Whether Dinah was held captive against her will, tried to make the best of it, or had similar affections for Shechem, we don't know. ♂

Shechem and his father Hamor came to negotiate a potential marriage with Dinah, but Jacob's sons were scandalized because "he had committed an outrage in Israel by lying with Jacob's daughter, for such a thing ought not to be done" (34:7).

Both Hamor and Schechem sought to make things right. Hamor offered to grant intermarriage and settlement rights between the families (34:6, 8-10), while a more undisciplined Shechem offered to write a blank check, promising

> ⚐ **Rape and marriage:** Dinah may have thought that marrying Shechem
> was her best option. Later on, Israel would codify rules for just such a situation:
> Exod. 22:16-17 calls for a man who seduces a virgin to marry her and pay the
> going bride price, while Deut. 22:28-29 orders a man who rapes a virgin to pay
> the father 50 pieces of silver and marry the girl, with no option for later divorce.
> These rules seem horrid to modern ears, but they were considered to be social
> safeguards in a world where a woman's security depended on being married, and
> a rape would disqualify her from a more traditional marriage, or at least severely
> decrease her prospects.

anything Jacob asked in exchange for Dinah: "Whatever you say to me I will give" (34:11-12).

Whatever Jacob thought, his sons overruled him by "deceitfully" agreeing to the offer, but only if the men of Shechem agreed to be circumcised as the Hebrews were (34:13-17). Surprisingly, Hamor and Shechem were "pleased" by the brothers' offer (34:18). Perhaps they thought the loss of a foreskin was a small price to pay for peace with their new neighbors, and a lot cheaper than the wagonloads of gold and silver that Shechem had been willing to pay.

Schechem and Hamor persuaded the other men of the city to pay a personal phallic price by arguing that Jacob's clan would ultimately be absorbed into their community and increase its wealth: "Won't their livestock, their property and all their other animals become ours?" (34:23a). Against the odds, the men of the city agreed to be circumcised—but in a world without sterile knives, pain medicine, or antibiotics, the small operation would leave them severely indisposed, or worse, for some time.

This is where Simeon and Levi—Jacob's second- and third-born sons, and full brothers to Dinah—enter the story. Once the newly circumcised men of the city were incapacitated and unable to fight, the two brothers entered the city with swords drawn. They killed Hamor the king, Shechem the prince, and every other defenseless man. The other brothers then followed their bloody lead, kidnapping the women and children, taking Dinah from Shechem's house and absconding with both the surviving people and the wealth of the city. And so the brothers responded to the perceived rape of their sister by raping an entire city and taking its women captive so they could do the same to them.

Jacob's tongue was finally loosed, and he castigated Simeon and Levi for their actions, not so much for the immorality of it, but for the threat to the family's survival: "You have brought trouble on me," he said. Jacob reasonably feared that the family's bloody treachery would become known, and that the leaders of other cities would unite against them and take vengeance (34:30).

The hot-blooded sons, however, were so determined to preserve their honor that future consequences were irrelevant. Their defense is not rational, but emotional: "Should our sister be treated like a whore?" (34:31).

Jacob and company were in fact endangered. As they left town and moved on toward Bethel, the text says "a terror from God fell upon the cities all around them, so that no one pursued them" (35:5). Once again, God had to rescue a stubborn people who kept endangering their own heritage.

Can you imagine a more horrific act? Yet nothing more is said about it until ch. 49, when Jacob lay on his deathbed and had a word for each of his sons. After ruling out Reuben as leader of the clan, he turned to Simeon and Levi:

Simeon and Levi are brothers; weapons of violence are their swords. May I never come into their council; may I not be joined to their company—for in their anger they killed men, and at their whim they hamstrung oxen. Cursed be their anger, for it is fierce, and their wrath, for it is cruel! I will divide them in Jacob, and scatter them in Israel. (49:5-7)

Jacob's "prophecy" explains why the tribe of Simeon faded into oblivion (probably absorbed by Judah) and the tribe of Levi was given no permanent home other than scattered towns within other tribal territories.

For Reflection: *Had you ever noticed before how the actions of Reuben, Simeon, and Levi resulted in their later demotion from leadership positions? Can you think of modern examples in which someone's early lack of discipline came back to haunt them later in life?*

BLESSINGS GAINED
(vv. 8-28)

With the eldest three sons having disqualified themselves from leadership, Jacob turned to Judah, his fourth-born, as the future leader of the tribes. Despite the misstep of refusing to give his young son to his daughter-in-law Tamar and later fathering sons by her when he mistook her for a prostitute, Judah acknowledged his error and did what was right.

Judah had demonstrated leadership before. According to the narrator, Judah had stepped forward to save Joseph's life by suggesting they sell him to passing traders when the other brothers wanted to kill him (37:26-27). Later, Judah spoke up in defense of his brother Benjamin when standing before Joseph in the pharaoh's court, and volunteered to remain behind as a hostage (44:14-34).

As old Jacob prepared for his entire family to leave Canaan, he appointed Judah and his family to lead the caravan when they went into Egypt to settle in Goshen (46:28).

So, when it came time for Jacob to speak parting words to Judah, he said:

> Judah, your brothers shall praise you; your hand shall be on the neck of your enemies; your father's sons shall bow down before you. Judah is a lion's whelp; from the prey, my son, you have gone up. He crouches down, he stretches out like a lion, like a lioness—who dares rouse him up? The scepter shall not depart from Judah, nor the ruler's staff from between his feet, until tribute comes to him; and the obedience of the peoples is his. Binding his foal to the vine and his donkey's colt to the choice vine, he washes his garments in wine and his robe in the blood of grapes; his eyes are darker than wine, and his teeth whiter than milk. (49:8-12)

The narrator, writing many years later, knew that Judah's descendants would become the preeminent tribe in the south, and that one of his descendants would be David, remembered as Israel's greatest king. "Judah is a lion's whelp" inspired the later idea of a messiah as the "Lion of Judah" (Rev. 5:5), and the reference to the scepter and the ruler's staff are further references to royalty that would come from the tribe of Judah.

David established a dynasty that God promised would never end (2 Samuel 7), even though the country of Judah fell to the Babylonians. In time, this gave birth to the hope of a coming messiah, and Christians believe that promise was ultimately fulfilled through Jesus Christ, yet another descendant of Judah, through David.

The following verses speak briefly to the other brothers, offering only brief predictions or observations about each, with the exception of Joseph, who is the subject of vv. 22-26. Though Jacob's words were directed toward Joseph, in practicality they spoke to his two sons, Ephraim and Manasseh, who Jacob had officially "adopted" as his own (48:5). Their descendants became the largest of the northern tribes, with Ephraim as the unquestioned leader even though he was younger. ♟

That Joseph's two sons received blessings suggests that, though Judah became the leader, Joseph received the double share of inheritance due to the eldest. Joseph's blessing is also marked by several titles for God, as Jacob said he had been blessed "by the hands of the Mighty One of Jacob, by the name of the Shepherd, the Rock of Israel, by the God or your father, who will help you, by the Almighty (Shaddai) who will bless you with blessings of heaven above, blessings of the deep that lies beneath, blessings of the breasts and of the womb" (vv. 24-25).

⚓ **Another reversal:** Genesis is replete with stories of how younger sons gain
ascendancy over their older brothers, and Joseph's sons are no exception. When
he brought them to his father Jacob to ask for his blessing, Joseph positioned the
older son Manasseh in front of Jacob's right hand so he could receive the primary
blessing, with Ephraim at his left. Although Jacob's eyesight was too poor to
distinguish between them, he crossed his hands so that his right hand rested on
Ephraim, giving him the blessing of priority (48:1-20).

Scholars have noted that, since the traditions of the ancestors may have
been written during the early days of the monarchy, the emphasis on younger sons
getting the blessing may have been an intentional way of helping to justify why
David and Solomon, both younger sons, could become kings over Israel.

The chapter concludes with Jacob's death (49:33), and the final chapter
relates how Joseph took the lead in embalming his father for burial back in
Canaan (50:1-14), reassuring his brothers that they were truly forgiven (50:15-
21), and remaining in Egypt until his death at age 110 (50:22-26).

So it is that the stories of the ancestors come to an end. By hit and miss, by
hook and by crook, despite all obstacles, God's promise to Abraham came to pass.
The once-threatened promise of progeny was fulfilled with a vengeance in the
land of Egypt, where the Hebrews multiplied so greatly that they faced a different
kind of threat—but that is a story for another book. We call it Exodus.

> **For Reflection:** *Judah's actions do not reflect ideal behavior, yet the narra-
> tor depicted Jacob as blessing him above his other brothers. Why do you
> think Judah escaped criticism? Could his confession of wrongdoing have
> something to do with it?*

THE HARDEST QUESTION
Did Judah deserve to be the leader?

We have noted in the lesson that Reuben, Simeon, and Levi all did foolish or offensive things that disqualified them from leadership. That left Judah in the catbird
seat. But did he deserve it? Judah has at least one embarrassing story to tell.

The story is found in Genesis 38, which falls within the "Joseph novella"
(chs. 37–50), a long stretch devoted mainly to Joseph's adventures in Egypt.
Chapter 38 offers a "meanwhile, back at the ranch" view of what was going on
back in Canaan after Joseph was transported to Egypt.

Another purpose of the extended story from the Yahwist (J)—which seems to be on a different track from the main narrative—is to explain why it is that one of David's ancestors was a Canaanite. Another is to give Judah some air time, since he will become an ancestor of kings and his tribe will dominate the southern kingdom. Yet another purpose is that it's a rollicking tale that's too good not to tell.

The story begins with Judah moving away from the rest of the family and settling in low-lying hill country near Adullam, about 10 miles northwest of the family camp in Hebron. There he formed a neighborly friendship with a local man named Hirah (v. 1), and chose the daughter of a Canaanite named Shua to become his wife (v. 2).

We are not told the name of Judah's wife. This may be the narrator's way of highlighting Tamar, the story's heroine and the only woman named in the story. The role of Judah's wife, for the story's purpose, is limited to bearing three sons and later dying at an opportune time.

Although Judah took a Canaanite wife, he was not criticized for it, even as there would be no criticism for Joseph when he married an Egyptian woman (Gen. 41:45). Jacob was the last to seek a wife with family connections, and a later ban on Hebrews marrying outside the clan (see Josh. 23:12-13, Ezra 9–10, Neh. 13:23-29) had not yet developed.

Judah's wife bore three sons: Er, Onan, and Shelah (vv. 3-5). When the sons reached marriageable age, Judah followed custom and arranged for his oldest to marry a local woman named Tamar. At some point afterward, Er died. In a shockingly straightforward manner, the narrator bluntly says that Er "was evil in the eyes of Yahweh, and Yaweh killed him" (or, "caused him to die," v. 7).

The narrator doesn't tell us what was so evil about the man. His main concern is that there was no heir for Er. This was regarded as a terrible thing: all men sought to beget sons to carry on their name and inherit their property. A custom known as "Levirate marriage" decreed that if a man died without issue, his nearest brother was obligated to marry the widow and beget a son who would be considered a son of the deceased brother, in line to inherit whatever share of the family fortune would have come due to that brother. Refusing the obligation was considered shameful (Deut. 25:5-10).

The closest brother to Er was Onan, and Judah instructed him to "Go in to your brother's wife and perform the duty of a brother-in-law to her; raise up offspring for your brother" (v. 8). Knowing that any son born to Tamar would receive Er's share of the inheritance and thereby reduce his own share, Onan didn't want to get Tamar pregnant, so he practiced birth control by *coitus interruptus*, withdrawing before ejaculating (literally, "he wasted earthward," v. 9). This was considered to be an intentional and rebellious act of failing to do his duty.

Some Christian traditions, believing that birth control is wrong and that every sperm cell should have a shot at becoming a zygote, have called upon this text to condemn both masturbation and birth control ("Onanism" has been used as a term for masturbation), but that is not what the text is about.

The point is that Onan consciously refused to fulfill his obligation toward his dead brother. As a result, the text—again with no apologies—says that Yahweh regarded Onan's selfish behavior as evil, and killed him, too (v. 10).

Judah did not recognize the deaths of his sons as a divine punishment, but concluded instead that Tamar was jinxed. He did not want to take a chance on losing his only remaining son, so he sent Tamar back to her father's family until Shelah was old enough to marry (v. 11). This was inappropriate, because Judah remained legally responsible for her, and as Shelah grew older, it became clear that he had no intention of allowing Shelah to marry Tamar.

This left Tamar in a desperate situation. As a widow, and with no children, she faced a life of poverty and limited rights. Tamar needed a son, and the timely death of Judah's wife (v. 13) gave Tamar an opportunity for a deceit of her own.

Unwilling to accept a desolate future, Tamar disguised herself as a veiled harlot—possibly as a cultic prostitute—and pitched a tent near a crossroads Judah would commonly pass, guessing that he might be anxious for a sexual diversion (vv. 13-14).

Judah did seek to obtain Tamar's services, though he did not recognize her behind her veil (v. 15). Boldly, he said "let me come in to you" (v. 16a). Staying true to her charade, Tamar negotiated a price of one young goat (v. 16b-17), demanding that Judah leave his personal seal and his recognizable staff as a guarantee of later payment (v. 18a).

So, we are told, "he went in to her, and she conceived by him" (v. 18b). Once Judah was out of sight, Tamar packed up her tent and resumed her widow's dress (v. 19).

When Judah sent payment, the "prostitute" was gone, and Judah apparently chose to keep mum about the loss of his personal items (vv. 20-23).

Tamar faced both shame and triumph three months later, when her pregnancy became known. When Judah heard that his daughter-in-law had "played the whore" and gotten pregnant, he angrily declared that Tamar should be burned to death (v. 24), a penalty not called for in the Bible.

Before the execution could be arranged, however, Tamar sent Judah's staff and seal to him with the message: "It was the owner of these that made me pregnant . . . take note, please, whose these are, the signet and the cord and the staff" (v. 25).

Fully chagrined, Judah declared: "She is more in the right than I, since I did not give her to my son Shelah" (v. 26). Thus Judah took responsibility for Tamar and accepted her back into the family, though the narrator carefully notes that he did not have sex with her again.

The true significance of the story becomes apparent when Tamar gives birth to twins, and we are not surprised to learn that the one born second would became the most prominent. His name was Perez, and he was destined to become an ancestor of both David (Ruth 4:18) and Jesus (Matt. 1:3).

The story is a reminder that life cannot always be confined to a legalistic box. Neither Judah's nor Tamar's actions fit the rules of acceptable behavior, yet neither was condemned. Indeed Tamar was praised, and Judah—despite more than one questionable action—remained sufficiently in Jacob's good graces to be designated as leader of the family.

AFTERWORD

Genesis 12–50 compiles one memorable story after another, amazing tales about patriarchs and matriarchs to whom God gave an amazing promise. Despite the anarchs (including God and the patriarchs themselves) who threatened the promise time and again, the stories insist that God not only overcame every obstacle, but also fulfilled the promises in a way far beyond anything Abraham could have imagined.

Jacob's prediction that Judah's descendants would rule, fulfilled not only in David but also in Jesus, the "son of David," set a course that expands the potential family of God to include every person on earth—like sand on the seashore or stars in the sky.

Those of us who call ourselves followers of Jesus can count ourselves among the blessed, and for that we can be truly thankful.

APPENDIX 1

ABRAHAM'S FAMILY CONNECTIONS
Generation One: Abram/Abraham
(11:27/17:5)

One purpose of the ancestral stories is to relate ancient traditions about the origins of not only Israel, but also of their kin, many of whom turned into enemies.

When we think of Abraham's immediate family, let's first consider his nephew, Lot, who traveled with him to Canaan but separated from Abraham and moved to the area around Sodom when their combined flocks were too large to find pasture (13:8-13). We know that Lot was married and had two daughters who were betrothed to men of Sodom, but none of the women are named. When Lot's family fled Sodom as the city was being destroyed, his wife died (reportedly as punishment for looking back, 19:24-26), and the daughters' potential husbands apparently perished with the other people of Sodom.

Afraid that they might be harmed by others in the area, Lot and his daughters took refuge in an isolated cave. The story says that when his daughters despaired of having children with regular husbands, they conspired to get their father drunk and have sex with him on consecutive nights (19:31-36). Both became pregnant and bore sons. The older daughter named her son Moab (possibly meaning "from father," 19:37), and the younger named her son Ben Ammi ("son of my people," 19:38). The two sons reportedly became the ancestors of the Moabites and the Ammonites (see "Frenemies," in Appendix 2).

Although we've known from the beginning that Abraham was married to Sarai/ Sarah (11:29/17:15), they had been childless for many years. At Sarah's urging, Abraham fathered a son by Sarah's handmaid, Hagar (16:3). The narrative says that Hagar named the child Ishmael ("God hears," 16:7-15). Ultimately, Ishmael and Hagar were sent away from the camp, moving deeper into the Negeb, where Ishmael married an unnamed woman from Egypt, and had 12 sons (25:12-18), who are said to have become the ancestors of the Ishmaelites (Appendix 2).

When all hope seemed past, Abraham and Sarah had a son, whom they named Isaac ("he laughs," 21:1-3) at God's instruction. We'll learn more about Isaac's family below in Generation Two.

At some point—presumably after Sarah died—Abraham took another wife, whose name was Keturah (25:1). She reportedly gave birth to six sons: Zimram, Jokshan, Medan, Midian, Ishbak, and Shuah (25:2-6). Among these, Midian is most significant, as he was the putative ancestor of the Midianites (see Appendix 2).

ABRAHAM'S FAMILY CONNECTIONS
Generation Two: Isaac
(21:1-3)

Born to Abraham and Sarah in their old age, Isaac was apparently kept close and did not marry until he was 40 years old, when Abraham sent a servant to Haran to choose a wife for Isaac from among his extended family. The servant returned with Rebekah (24:67), whom Isaac promptly claimed as his wife and settled into his mother's tent.

Isaac and Rebekah were childless for 20 years, according to the story, before she was able to conceive, bearing twins: Esau (25:25) and Jacob (25:26). Though technically the youngest, Jacob conspired to obtain the elder brother's blessing.

The narrator appears to believe Esau was unworthy of the blessing, as he chose to marry local women instead of finding a bride back in Haran. Esau married at least three wives and possibly more: the traditions are confused. Two of the women were identified as Hittites: Judith and Basemath (26:34), who reportedly made life miserable for Rebekah. He also married a cousin, a daughter of Ishmael named Mahalath (28:9), possibly hoping to win favor with his parents by marrying someone from the family. Esau's genealogy also includes a Canaanite/ Hittite wife named Adah (36:2). Esau reportedly moved his family to a desert area south of the Dead Sea, where they gave rise to the Edomites (25:30; 36:1, 8, 19, 43), who were among Israel's fiercest enemies.

We will learn more about Jacob in Generation Three.

ABRAHAM'S FAMILY CONNECTIONS
Generation Three: Jacob
(25:16)

We note by now that multiple sons were born during each generation, but so far, just one son was chosen to inherit God's promises to Abraham and carry on the "blessed" line of Abraham's descendants, even though the Hebrews could have multiplied more quickly if all of the sons had inherited the blessing. That changes with the birth of Jacob's 12 sons, born to four different women.

Jacob left his father's home in Hebron and journeyed north to find refuge from Esau with Laban, his mother's brother, in Haran. He also found wives there, marrying Leah (29:21-25) and Rachel (29:26-30) in back-to-back weddings, paying their bride-price with 14 years of labor tending Laban's sheep.

Seeing that Leah was unloved, the narrator says, God quickly granted her four sons: Reuben, Simeon, Levi, and Judah (29:32-35).

Unable to conceive on her own, Rachel insisted that Jacob impregnate her handmaid, Bilhah, who in time gave birth to Dan and Naphtali (30:5-8).

Leah had stopped getting pregnant, so she demanded that Jacob follow suit and sleep with her handmaid Zilpah, who bore two sons, Gad and Asher (30:9-13).

Once again able to conceive, Leah gave birth to two additional sons, Issacar and Zebulun, along with the only daughter named in any of the patriarchal genealogies, Dinah (30:16-21).

Finally, Rachel was able to conceive, giving birth to Joseph (30:22-24), who immediately became Jacob's favorite. Sometime later, perhaps several years, Rachel conceived again and bore Benjamin (35:16-18), dying in childbirth.

These 12 sons all became inheritors of the promise and the eponymous ancestors of the classic 12 tribes of Israel. The actual number and names of the tribes varied over time, but tracing those changes is beyond the scope of this book.

We will not repeat the genealogies accorded to the sons in Generation Four, though we note that the previous expectation of marrying only within the family had ceased. So far as we know, all of Jacob's sons found their wives from the various ethnic groups that made up the Canaanites—with the exception of Joseph, whose wife was Egyptian.

Interested readers can request a digital copy of a chart summarizing this information (suitable for printing horizontally on 8 ½ x 14 inch paper stock) by emailing the author at cartledge@nurturingfaith.net.

APPENDIX 2

ISRAEL'S "FRENEMIES"

As shown in the previous appendix, traditions in Genesis hold that several important people groups who later interfaced with Israel were also descended from Abraham's family. Some basic information about each can be found below.

Moabites

The Moabites lived east of the Dead Sea, claiming territory from Mount Nebo to the Zered Brook. They were said to be descendants of Moab, born to Abraham's nephew Lot and his oldest daughter (Gen. 19:33, 37).

Representative stories of conflict between Moab and Israel:
Numbers 22–24
Josh. 24:9
Judg. 3:12-30
1 Sam. 14:47
2 Sam. 8:2

Representative prophecies against Moab:
Isaiah 15–16
Amos 2:1-3
Jer. 9:25-26, 48:1-47
Zeph. 2:8-11

Ammonites

The Ammonites lived in the Transjordan, northeast of the Dead Sea. The capital, Rabbah, is now the city of Amman, capital of Jordan. They were said to be descendants of Ben 'Ammi, the son of Lot by his younger daughter (Gen. 19:35, 38). Israel was instructed not to take the lands of Moab and Ammon, but to preserve them for the heritage of the sons of Lot (Deut. 2:19, 37; Judg. 11:15).

Representative stories of conflict between Israel and Ammon:
   Judg. 3:13, 10:6, 11:4-40
   1 Sam. 11:1-11, 12:12, 14:47
   2 Samuel 10
   2 Sam. 12:26-3
   2 Kgs. 23:13, 25:25
   2 Chron. 20:1-30, 24:26, 26:8, 27:5
   Neh. 2:10, 19; 4:3, 7

Representative prophecies against Ammon:
   Jer. 49:1-6
   Ezek. 21:20, 25:1-7
   Amos 1:13-15
   Zeph. 2:8-11

During the postexilic period, intermarriage with Ammonites was expressly forbidden (Ezra 9:1-2; Neh. 13:1, 23-31). Ammonites and Moabites were forbidden from entering "the assembly of the LORD," i.e., worship at the temple, "to the tenth generation" (Deut. 23:3).

Ishmaelites

The Ishmaelites were described as living east of Canaan, in northern Arabia. The kingdom of Kedar, named for Ishmael's second son, was mentioned in Assyrian and Babylonian documents. There is some evidence of intermarriage with Edomites (Genesis 36) and the sons of Keturah (Gen. 25:1-4, 1 Chron. 1:32-33). Islamic tradition holds that Arab peoples were descended from Ishmael: thus Arabic Muslims also consider themselves to be children of Abraham.

The names "Ishmaelite" and "Midianite" sometimes appear interchangeable. Both were noted as wide-ranging traders whose home base was in Arabia. Both Ishmaelites and Midianites are said to have bought Joseph and sold him into Egyptian bondage (Gen. 37:25-28, 39:1). The Book of Judges says that Gideon went to war with the Midianites, but asked for gold earrings from the plunder, "for the enemy had golden earrings, because they were Ishmaelites" (Judg. 8:24).

Little conflict is recorded between Israel and the Ishmaelites. Some Israelites intermarried with Ishmaelites, and persons of Ishmaelite ancestry served important functions in Israel's early monarchy, including Amasa, appointed by Absalom (and later David) as head of the armies (2 Sam. 17:25, see also 1 Chron. 27:30).

Midianites

Descendants of Midian, Abraham's son by Keturah, Abraham reportedly gave them an inheritance and sent them to live in "the east country" (Gen. 25:6). The "land of Midian" to which Moses repaired in Exodus 2 probably refers to an area in northwestern Arabia near the Gulf of Aqaba. Moses' wife Zipporah and his father-in-law Jethro were Midianites (Exod. 2:15-22).

Stories of conflict:
> Midianite elders joined King Balak of Moab in hiring Balaam to curse the Israelites (Num. 22:1-7).
> Midianites reportedly led Israel astray at Shittim, prompting Moses to seek their destruction (Num. 25:1-7, 16-18; 31:1-12).
> Midianites remained, however. Gideon waged war against them (Judges 7–8. See Ps. 83:9, 11; Isa. 9:4, 10:26).

Edomites

The Edomites, who lived south of the Dead Sea, were often said to be descendants of Esau, and were thought to be Israel's closest kin—and bitterest enemies.

Representative stories of conflict:
> Judg. 6:1–8:28
> 1 Sam. 14:47
> 2 Sam. 8:13-14
> 1 Kgs. 22:47
> 2 Kgs. 8:20-22; 14:7-10, 22; 16:16
> Psalm 137

Doeg the Edomite appears as a black-hearted ally of Saul who betrayed and murdered the priests of Nob (1 Sam. 21:7, 22:9-22). Many years later, Edomites were accused of joining the Babylonians in plundering Jerusalem.

Representative prophecies against Edom:
> Jer. 27:2-7, 49:7-22
> Obadiah 11–14
> Ezek. 35:1–36:15
> Mal. 1:2-5